101
frozen, decadent desserts,
drinks & treats

Nutritional Analyses: Calculations for the nutritional analyses in this book are based on the largest number of servings listed within the recipes. Calculations are rounded up to the nearest gram or milligram, as appropriate. If two options for an ingredient are listed, the first one is used. Optional ingredients or serving suggestions are not included.

Recipe Developers: Bob Warden, Andrea Schwob, Stephen Delaney, Euro-Pro Test Kitchen Team, and Vanessa Spilios
Editors: Bob Warden, Mona Wetter Dolgov
Graphic Designer: Leslie Anne Feagley
Photo Creative Director: Anne Sommers Welch
Photography: Quenton Bacon and Gary Sloan
Food Stylist: Michael Pederson

Published in the United States of America
by
Great Flavors LLC
New Hope, PA 18938
www.greatflavors com

ISBN 978-0-578-12635-7
Printed in Canada

introduction • The NINJA Mega Kitchen System • 4

chapter 1 • ice cream • 10

chapter 2 • fruit-based ice cream • 68

chapter 3 • low-calorie d'lites • 80

chapter 4 • milkshakes & coffee drinks • 98

chapter 5 • sorbets & ices • 120

chapter 6 • pops • 132

index • 143

The Ninja Mega Kitchen System
. . . . .

Combines the functions of many kitchen appliances —
Blender, Food Processor & Single-Serve
Blending All in One Professional Unit!

1500 watts/2 horsepower motor

Extra-large 72-ounce pitcher with blade assembly

Extra-large 56-ounce processor bowl with blade assembly

Dough blade attachment

Two single-serve blending cups with blade and to-go lids

The Ninja Is Revolutionizing the Way We Make Homemade Ice Cream

· · · · · ·

Everyone loves homemade ice cream, but it has always been cumbersome, difficult, and time-consuming to make at home. It requires either spending several hundred dollars on an automatic electric ice cream maker with a built- in condensing freezer or buying an ice cream churn and dealing with all of its salted ice problems plus 30 minutes of required hand cranking. Another unsatisfactory solution is freezing a container overnight, pouring in an ice cream mixture, and hoping the ice cream is produced in 20 minutes, before it gets too warm.

Homemade Ice Creams and Frozen Treats in Less Than One Minute!

Creating ice cream and frozen treats with the Ninja Mega Kitchen System makes homemade ice cream making simple. Just as the #1 Selling Ninja Kitchen System has revolutionized blending and food processing, Ninja has also become known for transforming the way families make ice cream at home. Previous Ninja cookbooks have introduced recipes for making fruit-based ice cream in 30 seconds. Now Ninja has created a new ice cream revolution: dairy and non-dairy ice creams in less than a minute. Many of the new Ninja ice cream recipes are created by simply using an instant pudding mix as a shortcut, with our recipes, then freezing the ingredients in ice cube trays and molds. Watch the transformation into delicious homemade, all-natural "frozen goodness." Add sweet and crunchy flavors with natural goodness or unusual mix-ins. Enjoy personalized ice creams, frozen yogurts, shakes, and frozen pops in less than 60 seconds! THE POSSIBILITIES ARE ENDLESS.

ice cream

Use whole milk, low-fat milk, skim milk, half-and-half, heavy cream, soy milk, coconut milk, almond milk, or even coffee to make homemade ice cream in minutes. It's fast and easy, because all of the ice cream recipes in this book use a shortcut made possible by the Ninja food processor.

Ice Cream Made Backwards: Traditionally, ice cream is cooked custard that has air churned into it while it freezes.

In the 1940s, a leading food manufacturer invented an instant pudding mix that did not require cooking to make the refrigerated pudding or custard. Now this 70-year-old food technology combined with the Ninja's powerful multi-blade technology makes it possible to freeze the ice cream custard or pudding first and then use the Ninja food processor to whip it into a delicious, soft ice cream. Using the instant pudding mix as a shortcut eliminates having to cook custard. Many top restaurants make homemade ice cream using costly machines to do the whipping. Now using the Ninja food processor's unique blade technology, you have a shortcut to create the same restaurant-quality ice cream in your home in less than a minute! We have not found another food processor that can make these recipes. Using your Ninja, just follow the recipes featured in this cookbook.

fruit-based ice cream

Those of you who have already been making frozen fruit-based ice cream in your Ninja know how simple it is to take any frozen fruit, combine it with your choice of dairy and a sweetener, if desired, and enjoy ice cream in 30 seconds. We have included additional fruit-based recipe ideas in this book.

low-calorie d'lites

You control what goes into your ice cream and frozen delights. This chapter is dedicated to reduced-calorie options. Every recipe is less than 101 calories per serving. The secret to low-calorie ice cream, shakes, ices, sorbets, and pops is using low-calorie dairy choices as well as less sugar or an artificial sweetener. Almost every recipe in this book can be reduced in calories by making these simple changes.

milkshakes & coffee drinks
. . . .

Most milkshakes are a combination of ice cream and a liquid dairy or non-dairy product, with fruit sometimes added, then blended to a drinkable thickness. Most of the milkshake and coffee drink recipes in this book use the same instant pudding shortcut to make an ice cream base for each recipe, and they are a fraction of the cost of those you would purchase in an ice cream store or coffee shop. You will see that mix-ins are popular for making shakes, too. Featured are some great ideas, but be inspired to create your own original versions.

sorbets & ices
. . . .

There is nothing better than the light crisp taste of a sorbet or water ice as an alternative to ice cream. The recipes in this book are designed to use the power and unique blade system of the Ninja food processor to create perfectly blended and frozen sorbets and ices. Fresh fruit is the base for all the recipes in this chapter. You will find recipes that use the trendy healthy "superfoods" such as acai berries and blueberries, as well as recipes with other fruits like watermelon, mango, lemons, grapefruit, cherries, peaches, and strawberries. Experiment to create your own unique exciting recipes.

pops
. . . .

This chapter features recipes that incorporate instant pudding mixes for making homemade pudding pops and fruit pops. The limitless world of mix-ins also applies to these instant-pudding-based ice cream pops. Enjoy the fun examples in this book. One of our favorites is the Chocolate Dirt (graham cracker dust) with gummy worms frozen into the pulverized graham cracker mixture. You will love getting creative making pudding pops.

Several fruit-based pops are just as simple to make. Simply use the Ninja's powerful blender to puree fruit combinations into perfectly smooth puree ready for the mold or to have mix-ins or pieces of fruit gently mixed into the recipe. You determine the amount of calories that go into these homemade pops by altering the recipe ingredients, same as the ice cream. The less sugar used, the lower the calories. You can make fruit pops with as few as 35 calories each, depending on the size of the mold.

Using Mix-Ins
for Unlimited Ice Cream Possibilities

· · · · · ·

While creating recipes for this cookbook, we discovered that most everyone loves adding favorite mix-ins to ice creams, frozen yogurts, and milkshakes. Ice cream and yogurt franchises with a large selection of topping choices have become immensely popular and mainstream, catering to the desire for variety in ice cream and drinks. This cookbook features more than 100 mix-in ingredients to add to ice cream creations. Almost all the recipes in this book incorporate one or more of the most popular mix-in items.

First, either freeze or refrigerate the ingredients. Immediately after removing from the refrigerator or freezer, place in the Ninja food processor and pulse into the ice cream. AVOID room temperature ingredients — you run the risk of the ice cream melting quickly. Peruse the recipes in this book and see how limitless the possibilities are. Create ice cream treats that are uniquely your own. Try the Mexican chocolate ice cream for a totally new ice cream experience.

Mix-Ins Make Your Dessert Complete

· · · · ·

candies
Kit Kat
Milky Way
peanut butter cups
peppermint patties
pralines
Snickers
white chocolate chips
yogurt-covered raisins

nuts
almonds
cashews
hazelnuts
macadamia nuts
peanuts
pecans
pine nuts
pistachios
unsalted soy nuts
walnuts

fruit (fresh/frozen)
bananas
dark raisins
dried cherries
figs
frozen blueberries
frozen cheesecake
frozen cherries
frozen dark cherries
frozen mangoes
frozen mixed berries
frozen peach slices
frozen pineapple chunks
frozen raspberries
frozen strawberries
frozen tropical fruit medley
frozen whole strawberries
lemon zest
lime zest

cakes/cookies
all-butter pound cake
almond-flavored biscotti
brownies
cheesecake
chocolate cake
chocolate chip cookies
cinnamon buns
cobblers
cream-filled sandwich cookies
fortune cookies
frozen pound cake
fudge mint cookies
gingersnap cookies
graham crackers
macaroons
mini cream puffs
oatmeal cookies
peanut butter cookies
premade original-flavor rice pudding
sugar cookies
tiramisu
vanilla wafer cookies
yellow cake mix

sauces/syrup/spreads
caramel sauce
chocolate fudge
chocolate hazelnut spread
cream cheese
creamy peanut butter
dulce de leche
honey
hot fudge sauce
maple syrup
marshmallow crème
orange marmalade
peanut butter
strawberry sauce

miscellaneous
brandy
candied yams
coffee
cognac
corn tortilla chips
dark chocolate hot cocoa mix
dark rum
espresso
granola
guanabana nectar
light rum
malted milk powder
mini pretzels
pumpkin puree
red wine
sweetened flake coconut
toffee bits
waffle cone
waffles
whole-milk ricotta cheese

White Chocolate Orange Creamsicle Ice Cream, 34

ice cream 1

basic chocolate ice cream 12
basic vanilla ice cream. 13
s'mores ice cream. 15
piña colada ice cream 17
caramel pretzel ice cream 19
pistachio macaroon ice cream. 21
crispety crunchety peanut butter ice cream 23
crunchy banana strawberry granola ice cream 25
hawaiian ice cream. 27
chocolate hazelnut ice cream 29
coconut rum raisin ice cream. 31
chocolate cherry cake ice cream 33
white chocolate orange creamsicle ice cream. 34
cannoli ice cream 35
white chocolate malted ice cream. 36
chocolate peanut butter ice cream 37
cookies & cream ice cream 38
strawberry cheesecake ice cream 39
mint chocolate ice cream. 40
mexican chocolate ice cream 41
chocolate caramel pecan pie ice cream. 42
hot chocolate marshmallow ice cream 43
dulce de leche ice cream. 44
black & white grasshopper pie ice cream 45
pumpkin cheesecake ice cream 46
pineapple upside-down cake ice cream. 47
cinnamon buns ice cream 48
chocolate brownie heaven ice cream 49
chocolate truffle ice cream 50
peanut butter cream pie ice cream 51
the kitchen sink ice cream 52
pomegranate nuts & spice ice cream 53
blueberry lemon shortcake ice cream 54
peach cobbler ice cream 55
oatmeal cookie ice cream 56
dulce de leche cheesecake ice cream 57
cake batter ice cream. 58
butterscotch rocky road ice cream 59
key lime lemon pie ice cream 60
coconut almond ice cream. 61
pistachio rice pudding ice cream 62
cookies & cream chocolate cheesecake ice cream 63
tiramisu ice cream 64
chocolate orange ice cream. 65
loaded pistachio ice cream 66
a hun-ny of a coffee ice cream. 67

Y ou can enjoy this basic chocolate ice cream for its own chocolaty goodness or use it as a base for adding your own favorite mix-in ingredients.

basic chocolate ice cream

YIELD: 1½ pints
SERVES: 6
PREP TIME: 7 minutes
CALORIES: 80 per 4-oz. serving

· · · · ·

ingredients

**2½ cups plus
2 tablespoons whole
milk, divided**

**1 package (3.4 ounces)
chocolate instant
pudding mix**

· · · · ·

mix-in options

**FROZEN
STRAWBERRIES
PEANUT BUTTER
FROZEN DARK
CHERRIES**

method

1. In a large mixing bowl, pour 2 cups of whole milk. Add the chocolate pudding mix into the milk. Lightly whisk the mixture using a wire whisk until dissolved, approximately one minute. Do not overmix or the mixture will thicken and not be easy to pour.

2. Pour the mixture into two standard ice cube trays, equally distributing between the two.

3. Place the ice cube trays in the freezer and freeze for eight hours or overnight.

4. In a Ninja 56-ounce food-processing bowl fitted with the standard blade attachment, place all the frozen chocolate ice cubes. Add the remaining ½ cup plus 2 tablespoons of whole milk. Using the crush function, process for 35 to 40 seconds.

5. Remove the lid, carefully remove the blades, and serve.

T his is the Ninja plain vanilla ice cream recipe that is simply delicious eaten plain or with your favorite topping. You can also use it as a base for creating your own unique recipes. After blending this basic ice cream, and before removing it from the food processor, simply add in your favorite mix-ins, and with just a few pulses you can create your own unique recipes.

basic vanilla
ice cream

YIELD: 1½ pints
SERVES: 6
PREP TIME: 10 minutes
CALORIES: 82 per 4-oz. serving

· · · · · ·

ingredients

**2½ cups plus
2 tablespoons whole
milk, divided**

**1 package (3.4 ounces)
vanilla instant
pudding mix**

**2 teaspoons vanilla
extract**

· · · · · ·

mix-in options

SNICKERS

KIT KAT

MILKY WAY

method

1. In a large mixing bowl, pour 2 cups of whole milk. Add the vanilla pudding mix into the milk. Lightly whisk the mixture using a wire whisk until dissolved, approximately one minute. Do not overmix or the mixture will thicken and not be easy to pour.

2. Pour the mixture into two standard ice cube trays, equally distributing between the two.

3. Place the ice cube trays in the freezer and freeze for eight hours or overnight.

4. In a Ninja 56-ounce food-processing bowl fitted with the standard blade attachment, place all the frozen vanilla ice cubes. Add the remaining ½ cup plus 2 tablespoons of whole milk and vanilla extract. Using the crush function, process for 35 to 40 seconds.

5. Remove the lid, carefully remove the blades, and serve.

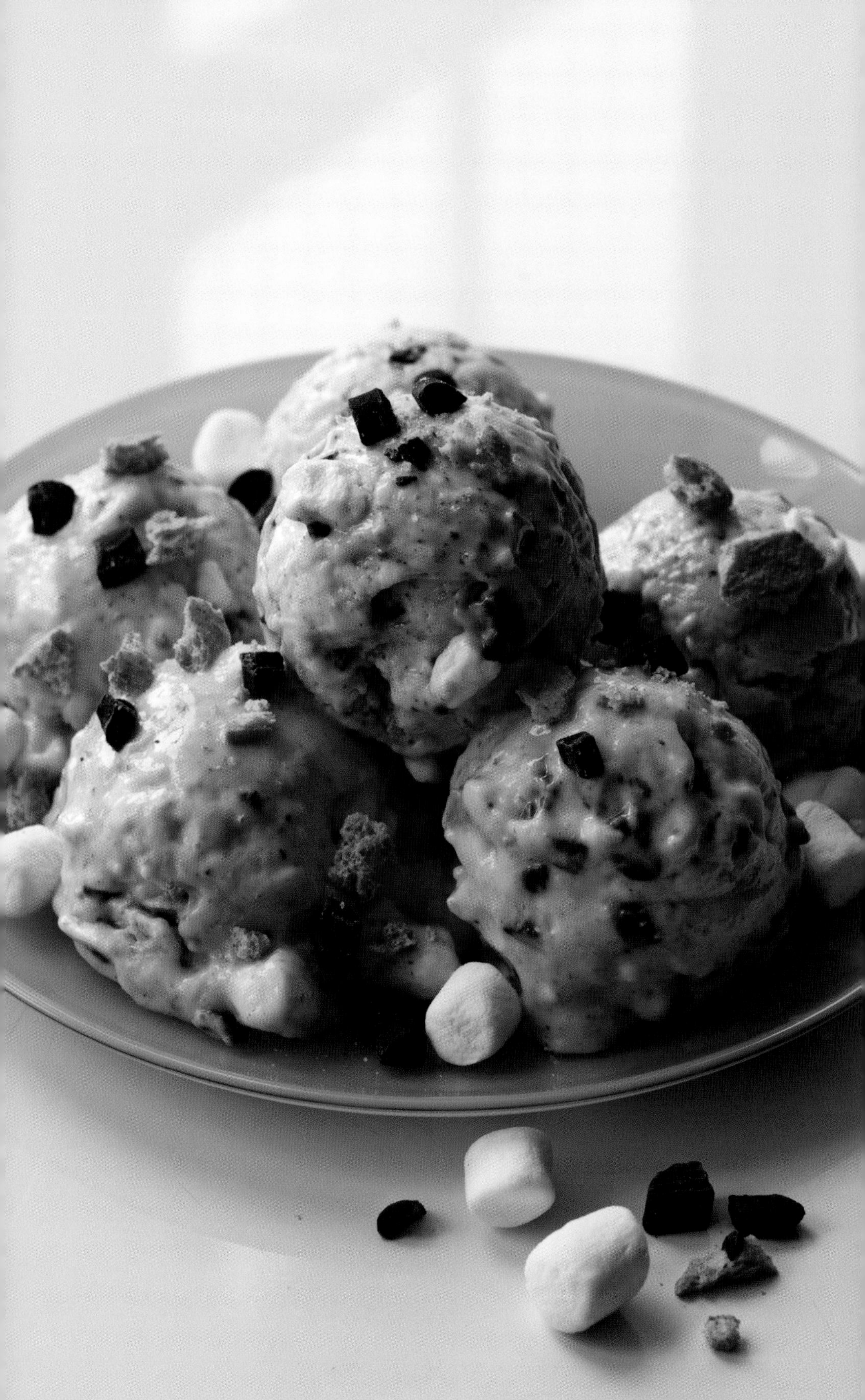

*T*he ice cream tastes like a campfire s'mores party. You can almost feel the bonfire.

s'mores ice cream

YIELD: 1½ pints
SERVES: 6
PREP TIME: 9 minutes
CALORIES: 420 per 4-oz. serving

· · · · · ·

ingredients

1⅓ cups half-and-half, divided

1 cup heavy cream

1 package (3.4 ounces) vanilla instant pudding mix

⅓ cup chocolate syrup

⅓ cup (2 ounces) semi-sweet mini chocolate chips

1 cup (2 ounces) mini marshmallows, frozen

1½ ounces graham cracker, broken into pieces

· · · · · ·

mix-in options

CARAMEL SAUCE
CARAMEL CHIPS
GRANOLA

method

1. In a large mixing bowl, pour 1 cup of half-and-half and the heavy cream. Add the vanilla pudding mix into the half-and-half and heavy cream mixture. Lightly whisk the mixture using a wire whisk until dissolved, approximately one minute. Do not overmix or the mixture will thicken and not be easy to pour.

2. Pour the mixture into two standard ice cube trays, equally distributing between the two.

3. Place the ice cube trays in the freezer and freeze for eight hours or overnight.

4. In a Ninja 56-ounce food-processing bowl fitted with the standard blade attachment, place all the frozen vanilla ice cubes. Add the remaining ⅓ cup of half-and-half, chocolate syrup, and semi-sweet mini chocolate chips. Using the crush function, process for 35 seconds.

5. Remove the lid and add the mini marshmallows and graham cracker pieces. Place the lid back on the food-processing bowl and crush for 15 seconds.

6. Remove the lid, carefully remove the blades, and serve.

P ineapple and rum! Whoever invented this combination deserves a gold medal because this is delicious.

piña colada ice cream

YIELD: 1½ pints
SERVES: 6
PREP TIME: 10 minutes
CALORIES: 132 per 4-oz. serving

· · · · · ·

ingredients

**2⅓ cups plus
1 tablespoon whole
milk**

**1 package (3.4 ounces)
coconut cream instant
pudding mix**

**6 ounces frozen
pineapple**

**2 tablespoons
light rum**

· · · · · ·

mix-in options

**TOASTED COCONUT
DRIED PINEAPPLE
FROZEN BANANAS**

method

1. In a large mixing bowl, pour 2 cups of whole milk. Add the coconut cream pudding mix into the milk. Lightly whisk the mixture using a wire whisk until dissolved, approximately one minute. Do not overmix or the mixture will thicken and not be easy to pour.

2. Pour the mixture into two standard ice cube trays, equally distributing between the two.

3. Place the ice cube trays in the freezer and freeze for eight hours or overnight.

4. In a Ninja 56-ounce food-processing bowl fitted with the standard blade attachment, place all the frozen coconut cream ice cubes. Add the frozen pineapple, the remaining ⅓ cup plus 1 tablespoon of milk, and the light rum. Using the crush function, process for 45 seconds.

5. Remove the lid, carefully remove the blades, and serve.

W ho doesn't like caramel and pretzels, soft and creamy with salty pretzel crunch?

caramel pretzel ice cream

YIELD: 1½ pints
SERVES: 6
PREP TIME: 10 minutes
CALORIES: 250 per 4-oz. serving

• • • • • •

ingredients

2½ cups whole milk, divided

1 package (3.4 ounces) butterscotch instant pudding mix

3 tablespoons caramel sauce

1 cup (1½ ounces) salted mini pretzels

⅓ cup (1¾ ounces) toffee bits

• • • • • •

mix-in options

**ICE CREAM CONE
PISTACHIOS
PEANUTS**

method

1. In a large mixing bowl, pour 2 cups of whole milk. Add the butterscotch pudding mix into the milk. Lightly whisk the mixture using a wire whisk until dissolved, approximately one minute. Do not overmix or the mixture will thicken and not be easy to pour.

2. Pour the mixture into two standard ice cube trays, equally distributing between the two.

3. Place the ice cube trays in the freezer and freeze for eight hours or overnight.

4. In a Ninja 56-ounce food-processing bowl fitted with the standard blade attachment, place all the frozen butterscotch ice cubes. Add the remaining ¼ cup of whole milk and caramel sauce. Using the crush function, process for 45 seconds.

5. Remove the lid and add the mini pretzels and toffee bits. Place the lid back on the food-processing bowl and using the pulse function, pulse 15 times.

6. Remove the lid, carefully remove the blades, and serve.

This is rich in pistachio and coconut flavor. The toasted coconut flakes give it an unusual crunch.

pistachio macaroon ice cream

YIELD: 1½ pints
SERVES: 6
PREP TIME: 13 minutes
CALORIES: 430 per 4-oz. serving

· · · · · ·

ingredients

2 cups coconut milk beverage

1 package (3.4 ounces) pistachio instant pudding mix

½ cup sweetened condensed milk

1 cup (2 ounces) sweetened flake coconut, toasted

· · · · · ·

mix-in options

**FORTUNE COOKIES
WAFFLE CONES
SUGAR COOKIES**

method

1. In a large mixing bowl, pour the coconut milk beverage. Add the pistachio pudding mix into the coconut milk beverage. Lightly whisk the mixture using a wire whisk until dissolved, approximately one minute. Do not overmix or the mixture will thicken and not be easy to pour.

2. Pour the mixture into two standard ice cube trays, equally distributing between the two.

3. Place the ice cube trays in the freezer and freeze for eight hours or overnight.

4. In a Ninja 56-ounce food-processing bowl fitted with the standard blade attachment, place all the frozen pistachio ice cubes. Add the sweetened condensed milk. Using the crush function, process for 35 seconds.

5. Remove the lid and add the toasted sweetened flake coconut. Place the lid back on the food-processing bowl and crush for 15 seconds.

6. Remove the lid, carefully remove the blades, and serve.

T his is the richest ice cream in this cookbook, but well worth the calories for a special occasion.

crispety crunchety peanut butter ice cream

YIELD: 1½ pints
SERVES: 6
PREP TIME: 9 minutes
CALORIES: 518 per 4-oz. serving

• • • • • •

ingredients

2½ cups half-and-half, divided

1 package (3.4 ounces) French vanilla instant pudding mix

¼ cup (2½ ounces) hot fudge topping

6¼ ounces crispety crunchety peanut butter candy, cut into 4 pieces

• • • • • •

mix-in options

**MARSHMALLOW
WAFFLE CONE
CHOCOLATE CHIPS**

method

1. In a large mixing bowl, pour 2 cups of half-and-half. Add the French vanilla pudding mix into the half-and-half. Lightly whisk the mixture using a wire whisk until dissolved, approximately one minute. Do not overmix or the mixture will thicken and not be easy to pour.

2. Pour the mixture into two standard ice cube trays, equally distributing between the two.

3. Place the ice cube trays in the freezer and freeze for eight hours or overnight.

4. In a Ninja 56-ounce food-processing bowl fitted with the standard blade attachment, place all the frozen French vanilla ice cubes. Add the remaining ½ cup of half-and-half and hot fudge topping. Using the crush function, process for 35 seconds.

5. Remove the lid and add the crispety crunchety peanut butter candy. Place the lid back on the food-processing bowl and crush for 20 seconds.

6. Remove the lid, carefully remove the blades, and serve.

T his is not low-calorie, but full of healthy energy and nutrition. You can reduce the calories by using low-fat granola.

crunchy banana strawberry granola ice cream

YIELD: 1¾ pints
SERVES: 6
PREP TIME: 12 minutes
CALORIES: 166 per 4-oz. serving

· · · · · ·

ingredients

1¼ cups nonfat Greek yogurt

1¼ cups plus
2 tablespoons whole milk, divided

1 package (3.4 ounces) banana cream instant pudding mix

3 ounces frozen whole strawberries

3 tablespoons honey

¾ cup granola

· · · · · ·

mix-in options

FROZEN RASPBERRIES
CHOCOLATE CHIPS
WAFFLE CONE

method

1. In a large mixing bowl, place the nonfat Greek yogurt and ¾ cup of whole milk. Mix for 10 seconds.

2. Add the banana cream pudding mix into the yogurt-milk mixture. Lightly whisk the mixture using a wire whisk until dissolved, approximately one minute. Do not overmix or the mixture will thicken and not be easy to pour.

3. Pour the mixture into two standard ice cube trays, equally distributing between the two.

4. Place the ice cube trays in the freezer and freeze for eight hours or overnight.

5. In a Ninja 56-ounce food-processing bowl fitted with the standard blade attachment, place all the frozen banana cream ice cubes. Add the remaining ½ cup plus 2 tablespoons of whole milk, frozen strawberries, and honey. Using the crush function, process for 40 seconds.

6. Remove the lid and add the granola. Place the lid back on the food-processing bowl and crush for 13 seconds.

7. Remove the lid, carefully remove the blades, and serve.

T he nonfat Greek yogurt is healthy, and the pineapple chunks, toasted coconut flakes, and nuts give this yogurt ice cream a distinct flavor and texture.

hawaiian ice cream

YIELD: 1¾ pints
SERVES: 6
PREP TIME: 13 minutes
CALORIES: 194 per 4-oz. serving

· · · · · ·

ingredients

1¼ cups nonfat Greek yogurt

1¼ cups plus 2 tablespoons whole milk, divided

1 package (3.4 ounces) vanilla instant pudding mix

4 ounces frozen pineapple chunks

¼ cup (¾ ounce) sweetened flake coconut, toasted

½ cup (2½ ounces) macadamia nuts, roasted, salted

· · · · · ·

mix-in options

**DRIED PAPAYA
DRIED MANGO
FROZEN MANGO**

method

1. In a large mixing bowl, place the nonfat Greek yogurt and ¾ cup of whole milk. Mix for 10 seconds.

2. Add the vanilla pudding mix into the yogurt-milk mixture. Lightly whisk the mixture using a wire whisk until dissolved, approximately one minute. Do not overmix or the mixture will thicken and not be easy to pour.

3. Pour the mixture into two standard ice cube trays, equally distributing between the two.

4. Place the ice cube trays in the freezer and freeze for eight hours or overnight.

5. In a Ninja 56-ounce food-processing bowl fitted with the standard blade attachment, place all the frozen vanilla ice cubes. Add the remaining ½ cup plus 2 tablespoons of whole milk and frozen pineapple. Using the crush function, process for 40 seconds.

6. Remove the lid and add the toasted sweetened flake coconut and macadamia nuts. Place the lid back on the food-processing bowl and crush for 18 seconds.

7. Remove the lid, carefully remove the blades, and serve.

H azelnut spread is one of the most delicious treats in the world. Make it into an ice cream and add some hazelnut crunch and you will WOW your guests!

chocolate hazelnut ice cream

YIELD: 1½ pints
SERVES: 6
PREP TIME: 12 minutes
CALORIES: 445 per 4-oz. serving

· · · · · ·

ingredients

2 cups skim milk

1 package (3.9 ounces) chocolate instant pudding mix

⅔ cup (7 ounces) chocolate hazelnut spread

⅓ cup (1¼ ounces) hazelnuts, toasted

· · · · · ·

mix-in options

TOASTED COCONUT
STRAWBERRY JAM
CHOCOLATE CHIPS

method

1. In a large mixing bowl, pour the skim milk. Add the chocolate pudding mix into the skim milk. Lightly whisk the mixture using a wire whisk until dissolved, approximately one minute. Do not overmix or the mixture will thicken and not be easy to pour.

2. Pour the mixture into two standard ice cube trays, equally distributing between the two.

3. Place the ice cube trays in the freezer and freeze for eight hours or overnight.

4. In a Ninja 56-ounce food-processing bowl fitted with the standard blade attachment, place all the frozen chocolate ice cubes. Add the chocolate hazelnut spread. Using the crush function, process for 45 seconds.

5. Remove the lid and add the hazelnuts. Place the lid back on the food-processing bowl and crush for 10 seconds.

6. Remove the lid, carefully remove the blades, and serve.

E*very bite of this ice cream is full of sweet raisin richness. If you don't like coconut, you can make this with any of your favorite milk products instead of coconut milk.*

coconut rum raisin ice cream

YIELD: 1½ pints
SERVES: 6
PREP TIME: 10 minutes
CALORIES: 155 per 4-oz. serving

· · · · · ·

ingredients

2⅔ cups coconut milk beverage

1 package (3.4 ounces) coconut cream instant pudding mix

3 ounces dark raisins

⅓ cup dark rum

2 teaspoons vanilla extract

· · · · · ·

mix-in options

TOASTED COCONUT
CARAMEL SAUCE
GOLDEN RAISINS

method

1. In a large mixing bowl, pour 2 cups of coconut milk beverage. Add the coconut cream pudding mix into the coconut milk beverage. Lightly whisk the mixture using a wire whisk until dissolved, approximately one minute. Do not overmix or the mixture will thicken and not be easy to pour.

2. Pour the mixture into two standard ice cube trays, equally distributing between the two.

3. Place the ice cube trays in the freezer and freeze for eight hours or overnight.

4. Place the dark raisins into a storage container and add the dark rum. Refrigerate for 24 hours.

5. In a Ninja 56-ounce food-processing bowl fitted with the standard blade attachment, place all the frozen coconut cream ice cubes. Strain and save the liquid from the soaked raisins. Add the remaining ⅔ cup of coconut milk beverage, the drained raisin liquid, and the vanilla extract. Using the crush function, process for 25 seconds.

6. Remove the lid and add the soaked raisins. Place the lid back on the food-processing bowl and crush for 15 seconds.

7. Remove the lid, carefully remove the blades, and serve.

C hocolate cake, chocolate ice cream, and cherries, all in one delicious scoop.

chocolate cherry cake ice cream

YIELD: 1½ pints
SERVES: 6
PREP TIME: 15 minutes
CALORIES: 175 per 4-oz. serving

· · · · · ·

ingredients

2½ cups whole milk

1 package (3.9 ounces) chocolate fudge instant pudding mix

1¼ cups (8 ounces) frozen cherries

4 ounces chocolate cake, frozen, cut into ½-inch cubes

· · · · · ·

mix-in options

**RED VELVET CAKE
WAFFLE CONE
GRAHAM CRACKERS**

method

1. In a large mixing bowl, pour 2 cups of whole milk. Add the chocolate fudge pudding mix into the milk. Lightly whisk the mixture using a wire whisk until dissolved, approximately one minute. Do not overmix or the mixture will thicken and not be easy to pour.

2. Pour the mixture into two standard ice cube trays, equally distributing between the two.

3. Place the ice cube trays in the freezer and freeze for eight hours or overnight.

4. In a Ninja 56-ounce food-processing bowl fitted with the standard blade attachment, place only half of the frozen chocolate fudge ice cubes, the remaining ½ cup milk, and the frozen cherries. Using the crush function, process for 30 seconds.

5. Remove the lid and add the chocolate cake. Place the lid back on the food-processing bowl and crush for 10 seconds.

6. Remove the lid, carefully remove the blades, and serve.

Yum! Orange creamsicles are an American favorite. Combined with the white chocolate, it is wonderful!

white chocolate orange creamsicle ice cream

YIELD: 1½ pints
SERVES: 6
PREP TIME: 12 minutes
CALORIES: 131 per 4-oz. serving

• • • • • •

ingredients

2 cups half-and-half

1 package (3.56 ounces) white chocolate instant pudding mix

½ cup orange juice

2 tablespoons orange zest

• • • • • •

mix-in options

CHOCOLATE CHIPS
CHOCOLATE SAUCE

method

1. In a large mixing bowl, pour the half-and-half. Add the white chocolate pudding mix into the half-and-half. Lightly whisk the mixture using a wire whisk until dissolved, approximately one minute. Do not overmix or the mixture will thicken and not be easy to pour.

2. Pour the mixture into two standard ice cube trays, equally distributing between the two.

3. Place the ice cube trays in the freezer and freeze for eight hours or overnight.

4. In a Ninja 56-ounce food-processing bowl fitted with the standard blade attachment, place all the frozen white chocolate ice cubes. Add the orange juice and orange zest. Using the crush function, process for 35 seconds.

5. Remove the lid, carefully remove the blades, and serve.

T otally decadent and totally delicious. You are having your cone and eating it too in this zesty recipe.

cannoli ice cream

YIELD: 2 pints
SERVES: 8
PREP TIME: 12 minutes
CALORIES: 367 per 4-oz. serving

· · · · · ·

ingredients

1½ cups half-and-half, divided

1 cup heavy cream

1 package (3.4 ounces) French vanilla instant pudding mix

½ cup (4¼ ounces) whole-milk ricotta cheese

1 tablespoon orange zest

½ cup (3 ounces) semi-sweet mini chocolate chips

1¾ ounces waffle cone, broken into pieces

· · · · · ·

mix-in options

LEMON ZEST
ICE CREAM CONE
PRALINES

method

1. In a large mixing bowl, pour 1 cup of half-and-half and the heavy cream. Add the French vanilla pudding mix into the half-and-half and heavy cream mixture. Lightly whisk the mixture using a wire whisk until dissolved, approximately one minute. Do not overmix or the mixture will thicken and not be easy to pour.

2. Pour the mixture into two standard ice cube trays, equally distributing between the two.

3. Place the ice cube trays in the freezer and freeze for eight hours or overnight.

4. In a Ninja 56-ounce food-processing bowl fitted with the standard blade attachment, place all the frozen French vanilla ice cubes. Add the remaining ½ cup of half-and-half, whole-milk ricotta cheese, and orange zest. Using the crush function, process for 20 seconds.

5. Remove the lid and add semi-sweet mini chocolate chips and waffle cone pieces. Place the lid back on the food-processing bowl and crush for 15 seconds.

6. Remove the lid, carefully remove the blades, and serve.

W *hite chocolate and malted milk balls give this ice cream an old-fashioned ice-cream-shop malt flavor.*

white chocolate malted ice cream

YIELD: 1½ pints
SERVES: 6
PREP TIME: 9 minutes
CALORIES: 367 per 4-oz. serving

· · · · · ·

ingredients

1½ cups half-and-half, divided

1 cup heavy cream

1 package (3.56 ounces) white chocolate instant pudding mix

⅓ cup malted milk powder, original flavor

1 cup (3½ ounces) malted milk balls

· · · · · ·

mix-in options

**PEANUTS
CHOCOLATE CHIPS
CHERRIES**

method

1. In a large mixing bowl, pour 1 cup of half-and-half and the heavy cream. Add the white chocolate pudding mix into the half-and-half and heavy cream mixture. Lightly whisk the mixture using a wire whisk until dissolved, approximately one minute. Do not overmix or the mixture will thicken and not be easy to pour.

2. Pour the mixture into two standard ice cube trays, equally distributing between the two.

3. Place the ice cube trays in the freezer and freeze for eight hours or overnight.

4. In a Ninja 56-ounce food-processing bowl fitted with the standard blade attachment, place all the frozen white chocolate ice cubes. Add the remaining ½ cup of half-and-half and malted milk powder. Using the crush function, process for 25 seconds.

5. Remove the lid and add the malted milk balls. Place the lid back on the food-processing bowl and crush for 15 seconds.

6. Remove the lid, carefully remove the blades, and serve.

*P*eanut butter and chocolate with hot fudge for extra
richness and peanut butter cups for crunch.

chocolate peanut butter ice cream

YIELD: 1½ pints
SERVES: 6
PREP TIME: 10 minutes
CALORIES: 400 per 4-oz. serving

. . . . . .

ingredients

1½ cups half-and-half, divided

1 cup heavy cream

1 package (3.9 ounces) chocolate instant pudding mix

2 tablespoons creamy peanut butter

3 tablespoons (1½ ounces) hot fudge topping

½ cup (3 ounces) peanut butter chips

. . . . . .

mix-in options

PEANUTS
CHOCOLATE CHIPS

method

1. In a large mixing bowl, pour 1 cup of half-and-half and the heavy cream. Add the chocolate pudding mix into the half-and-half and heavy cream mixture. Lightly whisk the mixture using a wire whisk until dissolved, approximately one minute. Do not overmix or the mixture will thicken and not be easy to pour.

2. Pour the mixture into two standard ice cube trays, equally distributing between the two.

3. Place the ice cube trays in the freezer and freeze for eight hours or overnight.

4. In a Ninja 56-ounce food-processing bowl fitted with the standard blade attachment, place all the frozen chocolate ice cubes. Add the remaining ½ cup of half-and-half, creamy peanut butter, and hot fudge topping. Using the crush function, process for 25 seconds.

5. Remove the lid and add the peanut butter chips. Place the lid back on the food-processing bowl and crush for 10 seconds.

6. Remove the lid, carefully remove the blades, and serve.

C ookies and ice cream go together in one dish in this crunch combination.

cookies & cream ice cream

YIELD: 2 pints
SERVES: 8
PREP TIME: 10 minutes
CALORIES: 256 per 4-oz. serving

· · · · · ·

ingredients

**1½ cups plus
2 tablespoons whole
milk, divided**

1 cup heavy cream

**1 package (4.2 ounces)
cookies and cream
instant pudding mix**

**3 ounces cream-filled
chocolate sandwich
cookies**

· · · · · ·

mix-in options

**MINT PATTIES
WHITE CHOCOLATE
CHIPS
FORTUNE COOKIES**

method

1. In a large mixing bowl, pour 1 cup of whole milk and the heavy cream. Add the cookies and cream pudding mix into the whole milk and heavy cream mixture. Lightly whisk the mixture using a wire whisk until dissolved, approximately one minute. Do not overmix or the mixture will thicken and not be easy to pour.

2. Pour the mixture into two standard ice cube trays, equally distributing between the two.

3. Place the ice cube trays in the freezer and freeze for eight hours or overnight.

4. In a Ninja 56-ounce food-processing bowl fitted with the standard blade attachment, place all the frozen cookies and cream ice cubes. Add the remaining ½ cup plus 2 tablespoons of whole milk. Using the crush function, process for 30 seconds.

5. Remove the lid and add the cream-filled chocolate sandwich cookies. Place the lid back on the food-processing bowl and crush for 10 seconds.

6. Remove the lid, carefully remove the blades, and serve.

S trawberry cheesecake flavor and richness with a crunch.

strawberry cheesecake ice cream

YIELD: 1¾ pints
SERVES: 6
PREP TIME: 12 minutes
CALORIES: 317 per 4-oz. serving

• • • • • •

ingredients

1 cup half-and-half

1 cup heavy cream

1 package (3.4 ounces) cheesecake instant pudding mix

4 ounces cream cheese

4 ounces frozen whole strawberries

1¾ ounces graham cracker, broken into pieces

• • • • • •

mix-in options

CHEEESECAKE RICE KRISPIES

method

1. In a large mixing bowl, pour the half-and-half and heavy cream. Add the cheesecake pudding mix into the half-and-half and heavy cream mixture. Lightly whisk the mixture using a wire whisk until dissolved, approximately one minute. Do not overmix or the mixture will thicken and not be easy to pour.

2. Pour the mixture into two standard ice cube trays, equally distributing between the two.

3. Place the ice cube trays in the freezer and freeze for eight hours or overnight.

4. In a Ninja 56-ounce food-processing bowl fitted with the standard blade attachment, place only half the frozen cheesecake ice cubes. Add the cream cheese and frozen whole strawberries. Using the crush function, process for 15 seconds.

5. Remove the lid and add the graham cracker pieces. Place the lid back on the food-processing bowl and crush for nine seconds.

6. Remove the lid, carefully remove the blades, and serve.

T his ice cream was "mint" to be eaten a little at a time. This recipe was also voted the creamiest ice cream in the book.

mint chocolate ice cream

YIELD: 1½ pints
SERVES: 6
PREP TIME: 10 minutes
CALORIES: 276 per 4-oz. serving

· · · · · ·

ingredients

**1½ cups plus
2 tablespoons whole
milk, divided**

1 cup heavy cream

**1 package (3.9 ounces)
chocolate fudge
instant pudding mix**

**⅛ teaspoon mint
extract**

**½ cup (3¼ ounces)
mint-flavored
chocolate candies**

· · · · · ·

mix-in options

**CHOCOLATE CHUNKS
MINI
MARSHMALLOWS**

method

1. In a large mixing bowl, pour 1 cup of whole milk and the heavy cream. Add the chocolate fudge pudding mix into the whole milk and heavy cream mixture. Lightly whisk the mixture using a wire whisk until dissolved, approximately one minute. Do not overmix or the mixture will thicken and not be easy to pour.

2. Pour the mixture into two standard ice cube trays, equally distributing between the two.

3. Place the ice cube trays in the freezer and freeze for eight hours or overnight.

4. In a Ninja 56-ounce food-processing bowl fitted with the standard blade attachment, place all the frozen chocolate fudge ice cubes. Add the remaining ½ cup plus 2 tablespoons of whole milk and mint extract. Using the crush function, process for 20 seconds.

5. Remove the lid and add the mint-flavored chocolate candies. Place the lid back on the food-processing bowl and crush for 10 seconds.

6. Remove the lid, carefully remove the blades, and serve.

T his recipe was voted by our recipe developers as their favorite ice cream in the book. You don't expect heat when you are eating ice cream. You get just enough here to add a great taste finish that lingers between bites.

mexican chocolate ice cream

YIELD: 1¾ pints
SERVES: 6
PREP TIME: 12 minutes
CALORIES: 409 per 4-oz. serving

. . . . . .

ingredients

**1½ cups plus
2 tablespoons whole
milk, divided**

1 cup heavy cream

**1 package (3.9 ounces)
chocolate fudge
instant pudding mix**

**½ teaspoon ground
cinnamon**

**¼ teaspoon cayenne
pepper**

**⅓ cup (1 ounce) sliced
almonds, toasted**

**1¼ ounces corn tortilla
chips, broken into
pieces**

. . . . . .

mix-in options

**PEANUT BUTTER
CUPS
MINT PATTIES
PEANUTS**

method

1. In a large mixing bowl, pour 1 cup of whole milk and the heavy cream. Add the chocolate fudge pudding mix into the whole milk and heavy cream mixture. Lightly whisk the mixture using a wire whisk until dissolved, approximately one minute. Do not overmix or the mixture will thicken and not be easy to pour.

2. Pour the mixture into two standard ice cube trays, equally distributing between the two.

3. Place the ice cube trays in the freezer and freeze for eight hours or overnight.

4. In a Ninja 56-ounce food-processing bowl fitted with the standard blade attachment, place all the frozen chocolate fudge ice cubes. Add the remaining ½ cup plus 2 tablespoons of whole milk, ground cinnamon, and cayenne pepper. Using the crush function, process for 20 seconds.

5. Remove the lid and add the toasted sliced almonds and corn tortilla chip pieces. Place the lid back on the food-processing bowl and crush for 10 seconds.

6. Remove the lid, carefully remove the blades, and serve.

P ecan pie is rich and crunchy, just like this ice cream. Not for the faint of heart!

chocolate caramel pecan pie ice cream

YIELD: 1½ pints
SERVES: 6
PREP TIME: 10 minutes
CALORIES: 244 per 4-oz. serving

· · · · · ·

ingredients

2⅓ cups whole milk, divided

1 package (3.9 ounces) chocolate instant pudding mix

¼ cup caramel sauce

4½ ounces pecans, toasted

· · · · · ·

mix-in options

GRAHAM CRACKERS
CARAMEL PIECES
CASHEWS

method

1. In a large mixing bowl, pour 2 cups of whole milk. Add the chocolate pudding mix into the milk. Lightly whisk the mixture using a wire whisk until dissolved, approximately one minute. Do not overmix or the mixture will thicken and not be easy to pour.

2. Pour the mixture into two standard ice cube trays, equally distributing between the two.

3. Place the ice cube trays in the freezer and freeze for eight hours or overnight.

4. In a Ninja 56-ounce food-processing bowl fitted with the standard blade attachment, place all the frozen chocolate ice cubes. Add the remaining ⅓ cup of whole milk and caramel sauce. Using the crush function, process for 40 seconds.

5. Remove the lid and add the pecans. Place the lid back on the food-processing bowl and crush for 10 seconds.

6. Remove the lid, carefully remove the blades, and serve.

C *hocolate and marshmallows go together every time. Rich and chocolaty with creamy marshmallow bites.*

hot chocolate marshmallow ice cream

YIELD: 1½ pints
SERVES: 6
PREP TIME: 12 minutes
CALORIES: 205 per 4-oz. serving

· · · · · ·

ingredients

**2¼ cups plus
2 tablespoons whole
milk, divided**

**1 package (3.9 ounces)
chocolate instant
pudding mix**

**2 packages (1.25 ounce
each) dark chocolate
hot cocoa mix**

**1½ cups (3 ounces)
mini marshmallows**

**⅓ cup (2 ounces) mini
semi-sweet chocolate
chips**

· · · · · ·

mix-in options

**FROZEN
STRAWBERRIES
PEANUTS
FROZEN DARK
CHERRIES**

method

1. In a large mixing bowl, pour 2 cups of whole milk. Add the chocolate pudding mix into the milk. Lightly whisk the mixture using a wire whisk until dissolved, approximately one minute. Do not overmix or the mixture will thicken and not be easy to pour.

2. Pour the mixture into two standard ice cube trays, equally distributing between the two.

3. Place the ice cube trays in the freezer and freeze for eight hours or overnight.

4. In a small mixing bowl, add the remaining ¼ cup plus 2 tablespoons of whole milk. Add the dark chocolate hot cocoa mix. Stir until dissolved. Set aside.

5. In a Ninja 56-ounce food-processing bowl fitted with the standard blade attachment, place all the frozen chocolate ice cubes. Add the dark chocolate hot cocoa and milk mixture. Using the crush function, process for 40 seconds

6. Remove the lid and add marshmallow and mini chocolate chips. Place the lid back on the food processing bowl and crush for 15 seconds.

7. Remove the lid, carefully remove the blades, and serve.

This recipe has only 114 calories of dulce de leche yumminess!

dulce de leche ice cream

YIELD: 1¼ pints
SERVES: 6
PREP TIME: 8 minutes
CALORIES: 114 per 4-oz. serving

· · · · · ·

ingredients

**2 cups plus
2 tablespoons vanilla-
flavored soy milk,
divided**

**1 package (3.4 ounces)
vanilla instant
pudding mix**

⅓ cup dulce de leche

· · · · · ·

mix-in options

**CARAMEL SQUARES
COFFEE BEANS
CARAMEL SAUCE**

method

1. In a large mixing bowl, pour 2 cups of vanilla-flavored soy milk. Add the vanilla pudding mix into the soy milk. Lightly whisk the mixture using a wire whisk until dissolved, approximately one minute. Do not overmix or the mixture will thicken and not be easy to pour.

2. Pour the mixture into two standard ice cube trays, equally distributing between the two.

3. Place the ice cube trays in the freezer and freeze for eight hours or overnight.

4. In a Ninja 56-ounce food-processing bowl fitted with the standard blade attachment, place half of the frozen vanilla ice cubes. Evenly distribute the dulce de leche throughout, then add the remaining half of the frozen vanilla ice cubes. Pour the remaining 2 tablespoons of vanilla-flavored soy milk. Using the crush function, process for 40 seconds.

5. Remove the lid, carefully remove the blades, and serve.

If you close your eyes, you will swear this ice cream is green. The cookies and cream combined with the mint cookies and peppermint patties leave your mouth feeling fresh and sweet.

black & white grasshopper pie ice cream

YIELD: 1½ pints
SERVES: 6
PREP TIME: 10 minutes
CALORIES: 220 per 4-oz. serving

· · · · · ·

ingredients

**2¼ cups plus
1 tablespoon whole
milk, divided**

**1 package (4.2 ounces)
cookies and cream
instant pudding mix**

**2 ounces fudge mint
cookies**

**4½ ounces peppermint
patties, frozen**

· · · · · ·

mix-in options

**FORTUNE COOKES
CHOCOLATE CHIPS
CRÈME D'MENTHE**

method

1. In a large mixing bowl, pour 2 cups of whole milk. Add the cookies and cream pudding mix into the milk. Lightly whisk the mixture using a wire whisk until dissolved, approximately one minute. Do not overmix or the mixture will thicken and not be easy to pour.

2. Pour the mixture into two standard ice cube trays, equally distributing between the two.

3. Place the ice cube trays in the freezer and freeze for eight hours or overnight.

4. In a Ninja 56-ounce food-processing bowl fitted with the standard blade attachment, place all the frozen cookies and cream ice cubes. Add the remaining ¼ cup plus 1 tablespoon of whole milk. Using the crush function, process for 30 seconds.

5. Remove the lid and add fudge mint cookies and frozen peppermint patties. Place the lid back on the food-processing bowl and crush for 20 seconds.

6. Remove the lid, carefully remove the blades, and serve.

Pumpkin cheesecake flavor with added nutmeg and cinnamon to give it extra flavor.

pumpkin cheesecake ice cream

YIELD: 2 pints
SERVES: 6
PREP TIME: 14 minutes
CALORIES: 254 per 4-oz. serving

· · · · · ·

ingredients

2¼ cups half-and-half, divided

1 package (3.4 ounces) cheesecake instant pudding mix

1 cheesecake (6 ounces), frozen

1 cup (8 ounces) pumpkin puree

½ teaspoon ground nutmeg

¾ teaspoon ground cinnamon

· · · · · ·

mix-in options

**GRAHAM CRACKERS
WAFFLE CONE
LEMON ZEST**

method

1. In a large mixing bowl, pour 2 cups of half-and-half. Add the cheesecake pudding mix into the half-and-half. Lightly whisk the mixture using a wire whisk until dissolved, approximately one minute. Do not overmix or the mixture will thicken and not be easy to pour.

2. Pour the mixture into two standard ice cube trays, equally distributing between the two.

3. Place the ice cube trays in the freezer and freeze for eight hours or overnight.

4. In a Ninja 56-ounce food-processing bowl fitted with the standard blade attachment, place all the frozen cheesecake ice cubes. Add the remaining ¼ cup of half-and-half, frozen cheesecake, pumpkin puree, ground nutmeg, and ground cinnamon. Using the crush function, process for 40 seconds.

5. Remove the lid, carefully remove the blades, and serve.

T his recipe puts good use to leftover cake. The cake adds a totally different texture and taste to ice cream.

pineapple upside-down cake ice cream

YIELD: 1½ pints
SERVES: 6
PREP TIME: 10 minutes
CALORIES: 307 per 4-oz. serving

· · · · · ·

ingredients

2½ cups half-and-half, divided

1 package (3.4 ounces) butterscotch instant pudding mix

8 ounces frozen pineapple chunks

3 ounces all-butter pound cake, frozen, cut into 1-inch cubes

· · · · · ·

mix-in options

DRIED PINEAPPLE
CARAMEL SAUCE
DRIED MANGO

method

1. In a large mixing bowl, pour 2 cups of half-and-half. Add the butterscotch pudding mix into the half-and-half. Lightly whisk the mixture using a wire whisk until dissolved, approximately one minute. Do not overmix or the mixture will thicken and not be easy to pour.

2. Pour the mixture into two standard ice cube trays, equally distributing between the two.

3. Place the ice cube trays in the freezer and freeze for eight hours or overnight.

4. In a Ninja 56-ounce food-processing bowl fitted with the standard blade attachment, place only half of the frozen butterscotch ice cubes. Add the remaining ½ cup of half-and-half and frozen pineapple chunks. Using the crush function, process for 40 seconds.

5. Remove the lid and add all-butter pound cake. Place the lid back on the food-processing bowl and crush for 15 seconds.

6. Remove the lid, carefully remove the blades, and serve.

T his will blow away anyone who loves cinnamon buns. You can make really great use of day-old cinnamon buns. Don't throw them away! Freeze them, and when you want an unbelievable ice cream treat, they will be ready and waiting.

cinnamon buns ice cream

YIELD: 1½ pints
SERVES: 6
PREP TIME: 10 minutes
CALORIES: 219 per 4-oz. serving

. . . . . .

ingredients

2⅔ cups half-and-half, divided

1 package (3.4 ounces) French vanilla instant pudding mix

3½ ounces cinnamon buns, frozen, cut into 1-inch cubes

¾ teaspoon ground cinnamon

. . . . . .

mix-in options

**CARAMEL SAUCE
DULCE DE LECHE
ICE CREAM CONE**

method

1. In a large mixing bowl, pour 2 cups of half-and-half. Add the French vanilla pudding mix into the half-and-half. Lightly whisk the mixture using a wire whisk until dissolved, approximately one minute. Do not overmix or the mixture will thicken and not be easy to pour.

2. Pour the mixture into two standard ice cube trays, equally distributing between the two.

3. Place the ice cube trays in the freezer and freeze for eight hours or overnight.

4. In a Ninja 56-ounce food-processing bowl fitted with the standard blade attachment, place all the frozen French vanilla ice cubes. Add the remaining ⅔ cup of half-and-half. Using the crush function, process for 30 seconds.

5. Remove the lid and add the cinnamon buns and ground cinnamon. Place the lid back on the food-processing bowl and crush for 15 seconds.

6. Remove the lid, carefully remove the blades, and serve.

The title of this recipe says it all. With these scrumptious ingredients, you can't go wrong.

chocolate brownie heaven ice cream

YIELD: 1½ pints
SERVES: 6
PREP TIME: 12 minutes
CALORIES: 326 per 4-oz. serving

· · · · · ·

ingredients

2⅔ cups half-and-half, divided

1 package (3.9 ounces) chocolate fudge instant pudding mix

4 ounces brownies, refrigerated, cut into 1-inch cubes

¾ cup (3 ounces) walnuts, toasted

· · · · · ·

mix-in options

CHOCOLATE FUDGE
PEANUTS
DRIED CHERRIES

method

1. In a large mixing bowl, pour 2 cups of half-and-half. Add the chocolate fudge pudding mix into the half-and-half. Lightly whisk the mixture using a wire whisk until dissolved, approximately one minute. Do not overmix or the mixture will thicken and not be easy to pour.

2. Pour the mixture into two standard ice cube trays, equally distributing between the two.

3. Place the ice cube trays in the freezer and freeze for eight hours or overnight.

4. In a Ninja 56-ounce food-processing bowl fitted with the standard blade attachment, place all the frozen chocolate fudge ice cubes. Add the remaining ⅔ cup of half-and-half. Using the crush function, process for 30 seconds.

5. Remove the lid and add the brownies and walnuts. Place the lid back on the food-processing bowl and crush for 15 seconds.

6. Remove the lid, carefully remove the blades, and serve.

D ouble truffle trouble with this mouthwatering treat. Great as the ultimate after-dinner treat.

chocolate truffle ice cream

YIELD: 1½ pints
SERVES: 6
PREP TIME: 8 minutes
CALORIES: 244 per 4-oz. serving

. . . . . .

ingredients

2⅔ cups half-and-half, divided

1 package (3.9 ounces) chocolate fudge instant pudding mix

3¾ ounces chocolate truffles, frozen

. . . . . .

mix-in options

CHOCOLATE CHIPS
CHOCOLATE SAUCE

method

1. In a large mixing bowl, pour 2 cups of half-and-half. Add the chocolate fudge pudding mix into the half-and-half. Lightly whisk the mixture using a wire whisk until dissolved, approximately one minute. Do not overmix or the mixture will thicken and not be easy to pour.

2. Pour the mixture into two standard ice cube trays, equally distributing between the two.

3. Place the ice cube trays in the freezer and freeze for eight hours or overnight.

4. In a Ninja 56-ounce food-processing bowl fitted with the standard blade attachment, place all the frozen chocolate fudge ice cubes. Add the remaining ⅔ cup of half-and-half. Using the crush function, process for 40 seconds.

5. Remove the lid and add the chocolate truffles. Place the lid back on the food-processing bowl and crush for 20 seconds.

6. Remove the lid, carefully remove the blades, and serve.

I f you like peanut butter, you will love this combination of cookies and peanut butter with some added crunch.

peanut butter cream pie ice cream

YIELD: 1½ pints
SERVES: 6
PREP TIME: 11 minutes
CALORIES: 334 per 4-oz. serving

· · · · · ·

ingredients

2½ cups half-and-half, divided

1 package (4.2 ounces) cookies and cream instant pudding mix

½ cup creamy peanut butter

3½ ounces peanut butter cups, frozen

· · · · · ·

mix-in options

PEANUTS
CHOCOLATE SAUCE

method

1. In a large mixing bowl, pour 2 cups of half-and-half. Add the cookies and cream pudding mix into the half-and-half. Lightly whisk the mixture using a wire whisk until dissolved, approximately one minute. Do not overmix or the mixture will thicken and not be easy to pour.

2. Pour the mixture into two standard ice cube trays, equally distributing between the two.

3. Place the ice cube trays in the freezer and freeze for eight hours or overnight.

4. In a Ninja 56-ounce food-processing bowl fitted with the standard blade attachment, place all the frozen cookies and cream ice cubes. Add the remaining ½ cup of half-and-half and peanut butter. Using the crush function, process for 30 seconds.

5. Remove the lid and add the peanut butter cups. Place the lid back on the food-processing bowl and crush for 10 seconds.

6. Remove the lid, carefully remove the blades, and serve.

This recipe was designed for lots of sweetness and crunch, and it delivers!

the kitchen sink ice cream

YIELD: 2 pints
SERVES: 8
PREP TIME: 12 minutes
CALORIES: 216 per 4-oz. serving

• • • • • •

ingredients

2⅓ **cups half-and-half, divided**

1 **package (3.4 ounces) banana cream instant pudding mix**

⅓ **cup caramel sauce**

¾ **cup (1 ounce) mini pretzels**

⅔ **cup (2 ounces) walnuts, toasted**

1 **ounce waffle cone**

• • • • • •

mix-in options

**FROZEN BANANAS
MARACHINO
CHERRIES
FROZEN WAFFLES**

method

1. In a large mixing bowl, pour 2 cups of half-and-half. Add the banana cream pudding mix into the half-and-half. Lightly whisk the mixture using a wire whisk until dissolved, approximately one minute. Do not overmix or the mixture will thicken and not be easy to pour.

2. Pour the mixture into two standard ice cube trays, equally distributing between the two.

3. Place the ice cube trays in the freezer and freeze for eight hours or overnight.

4. In a Ninja 56-ounce food-processing bowl fitted with the standard blade attachment, place all the frozen banana cream ice cubes. Add the remaining ⅓ cup of half-and-half and caramel sauce. Using the crush function, process for 30 seconds.

5. Remove the lid and add the mini pretzels, walnuts, and waffle cone. Place the lid back on the food-processing bowl and crush for 25 seconds.

6. Remove the lid, carefully remove the blades, and serve.

J ust more than 100 calories per serving, this pomegranate ice cream has a real kick to it.

pomegranate nuts & spice ice cream

YIELD: 1¾ pints
SERVES: 6
PREP TIME: 13 minutes
CALORIES: 127 per 4-oz. serving

· · · · · ·

ingredients

1½ cup nonfat Greek yogurt

1 cup whole milk

1 package (3.56 ounces) white chocolate instant pudding mix

½ cup pomegranate blueberry juice

¼ teaspoon cayenne pepper

½ teaspoon ground nutmeg

½ cup (4 ounces) dark-chocolate-coated pomegranate

⅓ cup (1⅛ ounces) unsalted soy nuts

· · · · · ·

mix-in options

CHOCOLATE SYRUP
PEANUTS
PISTACHIOS

method

1. In a large mixing bowl, place 1 cup of nonfat Greek yogurt and the whole milk. Mix for 10 seconds.

2. Add the white chocolate pudding mix into the yogurt-milk mixture. Lightly whisk the mixture using a wire whisk until dissolved, approximately one minute. Do not overmix or the mixture will thicken and not be easy to pour.

3. Pour the mixture into two standard ice cube trays, equally distributing between the two.

4. Place the ice cube trays in the freezer and freeze for eight hours or overnight.

5. In a Ninja 56-ounce food-processing bowl fitted with the standard blade attachment, place all the frozen white chocolate ice cubes. Add the remaining ½ cup of nonfat Greek yogurt, pomegranate blueberry juice, cayenne pepper, and ground nutmeg. Using the crush function, process for 40 seconds.

6. Remove the lid and add the dark-chocolate-coated pomegranate and unsalted soy nuts. Place the lid back on the food-processing bowl and crush for 15 seconds.

7. Remove the lid, carefully remove the blades, and serve.

Y ou can substitute shortcake cookies for the sugar cookies for an even richer butter flavor.

blueberry lemon shortcake ice cream

YIELD: 2 pints
SERVES: 8
PREP TIME: 13 minutes
CALORIES: 164 per 4-oz. serving

. . . . . .

ingredients

1¼ cups nonfat Greek yogurt

1 cup whole milk

1 package (3.4 ounces) lemon instant pudding mix

8 ounces frozen blueberries

1 cup blueberry cultured-milk smoothie

2 tablespoons lemon zest

2¾ ounces sugar cookies, broken into pieces

. . . . . .

mix-in options

BLUEBERRY JAM
EXTRA BLUEBERRIES
YOGURT-COVERED BERRIES

method

1. In a large mixing bowl, place the nonfat Greek yogurt and whole milk. Mix for 10 seconds.

2. Add the lemon pudding mix into the yogurt-milk mixture. Lightly whisk the mixture using a wire whisk until dissolved, approximately one minute. Do not overmix or the mixture will thicken and not be easy to pour.

3. Pour the mixture into two standard ice cube trays, equally distributing between the two.

4. Place the ice cube trays in the freezer and freeze for eight hours or overnight.

5. In a Ninja 56-ounce food-processing bowl fitted with the standard blade attachment, place only half of the frozen lemon ice cubes. Add frozen blueberries, blueberry cultured-milk smoothie, and lemon zest. Using the crush function, process for 35 seconds.

6. Remove the lid and add the sugar cookies. Place the lid back on the food-processing bowl and crush for 20 seconds.

7. Remove the lid, carefully remove the blades, and serve.

The peach and apricot cookies make this recipe delicious. If you can't find these cookies, no worries — substitute your favorite fruit cookies and fresh fruit.

peach cobbler ice cream

YIELD: 2 pints
SERVES: 8
PREP TIME: 12 minutes
CALORIES: 159 per 4-oz. serving

• • • • • •

ingredients

1½ **cups nonfat Greek yogurt**

¾ **cup whole milk**

1 **package (3.4 ounces) vanilla instant pudding mix**

8 **ounces frozen sliced peaches**

¾ **cup half-and-half**

2 **tablespoons light brown sugar**

6 **ounces sweet peach and apricot cookies, broken into pieces**

• • • • • •

mix-in options

**DRIED PEACHES
CARAMEL SAUCE
WAFFLE CONE**

method

1. In a large mixing bowl, place the nonfat Greek yogurt and the whole milk. Mix for 10 seconds.

2. Add the vanilla pudding mix into the yogurt-milk mixture. Lightly whisk the mixture using a wire whisk until dissolved, approximately one minute. Do not overmix or the mixture will thicken and not be easy to pour.

3. Pour the mixture into two standard ice cube trays, equally distributing between the two.

4. Place the ice cube trays in the freezer and freeze for eight hours or overnight.

5. In a Ninja 56-ounce food-processing bowl fitted with the standard blade attachment, place only half of the frozen vanilla ice cubes. Add frozen sliced peaches, half-and-half, and light brown sugar. Using the crush function, process for 25 seconds.

6. Remove the lid and add the sweet peach and apricot cookies. Place the lid back on the food-processing bowl and crush for 10 seconds.

7. Remove the lid, carefully remove the blades, and serve.

A yogurt ice cream you won't find in your local frozen yogurt shop!

oatmeal cookie ice cream

YIELD: 1¾ pints
SERVES: 6
PREP TIME: 10 minutes
CALORIES: 245 per 4-oz. serving

· · · · · ·

ingredients

¾ cup nonfat
Greek yogurt

1¼ cup whole milk

1 package (3.4 ounces)
vanilla instant
pudding mix

1 cup plain low-
fat cultured-milk
smoothie beverage

1 teaspoon ground
cinnamon

3½ ounces oatmeal
cookies, broken into
pieces

¾ cup (5 ounces)
yogurt-covered raisins

· · · · · ·

mix-in options

DRIED FRUIT
CHOCOLATE CHIPS
ICE CREAM CONES

method

1. In a large mixing bowl, place the nonfat Greek yogurt and whole milk. Mix for 10 seconds. Add the vanilla pudding mix into the yogurt-milk mixture. Lightly whisk the mixture using a wire whisk until dissolved, approximately one minute. Do not overmix or the mixture will thicken and not be easy to pour.

2. Pour the mixture into two standard ice cube trays, equally distributing between the two.

3. Place the ice cube trays in the freezer and freeze for eight hours or overnight.

4. In a Ninja 56-ounce food-processing bowl fitted with the standard blade attachment, place all the frozen vanilla ice cubes. Add the low-fat cultured-milk smoothie beverage and ground cinnamon. Using the crush function, process for 40 seconds.

5. Remove the lid and add the oatmeal cookies and yogurt-covered raisins. Place the lid back on the food-processing bowl and crush for 15 seconds.

6. Remove the lid, carefully remove the blades, and serve.

B ecause of its caramelized sweetness, dulce de leche is used to flavor many candies. Now it flavors an unbelievably good cheesecake ice cream.

dulce de leche cheesecake ice cream

YIELD: 1½ pints
SERVES: 6
PREP TIME: 15 minutes
CALORIES: 203 per 4-oz. serving

· · · · · ·

ingredients

2 cups whole milk

1 package (3.4 ounces) cheesecake instant pudding mix

⅓ cup dulce de leche

4 ounces cream cheese, cut into ½-inch pieces

1 ounce graham crackers

· · · · · ·

mix-in options

BUTTERSCOTCH CHIPS
SUGAR COOKIES
CARAMEL SAUCE

method

1. In a large mixing bowl, pour the whole milk. Add the cheesecake pudding mix into the milk. Lightly whisk the mixture using a wire whisk until dissolved, approximately one minute. Do not overmix or the mixture will thicken and not be easy to pour.

2. Pour the mixture into two standard ice cube trays, equally distributing between the two.

3. Place the ice cube trays in the freezer and freeze for eight hours or overnight.

4. In a Ninja 56-ounce food-processing bowl fitted with the standard blade attachment, place half the frozen cheesecake ice cubes, then add the dulce de leche and cream cheese. Add the other half of the frozen cheesecake ice cubes. Using the crush function, process for 35 seconds.

5. Remove the lid and add the graham crackers. Place the lid back on the food-processing bowl and crush for 10 seconds.

6. Remove the lid, carefully remove the blades, and serve.

D efinitely a great way to have your cake and ice cream, too!

cake batter ice cream

YIELD: 1½ pints
SERVES: 6
PREP TIME: 10 minutes
CALORIES: 107 per 4-oz. serving

· · · · · ·

ingredients

2½ cups almond milk

1 package (3.4 ounces) French vanilla instant pudding mix

½ cup yellow cake mix

1 teaspoon vanilla extract

1 tablespoon sweetened condensed milk

· · · · · ·

mix-in options

**ALMONDS
VANILLA FROSTING
ICE CREAM CONE**

method

1. In a large mixing bowl, pour 2 cups of almond milk. Add the French vanilla pudding mix into the almond milk. Lightly whisk the mixture using a wire whisk until dissolved, approximately one minute. Do not overmix or the mixture will thicken and not be easy to pour.

2. Pour the mixture into two standard ice cube trays, equally distributing between the two.

3. Place the ice cube trays in the freezer and freeze for eight hours or overnight.

4. In a Ninja 56-ounce food-processing bowl fitted with the standard blade attachment, place half of the frozen French vanilla ice cubes. Evenly distribute the yellow cake mix throughout, and then add the remaining half of frozen French vanilla ice cubes. Add the remaining ½ cup almond milk, vanilla extract, and sweetened condensed milk. Using the crush function, process for 40 seconds.

5. Remove the lid, carefully remove the blades, and serve.

B utterscotch ice cream and marshmallows. Try it, you'll like it!

butterscotch rocky road ice cream

YIELD: 1½ pints
SERVES: 6
PREP TIME: 9 minutes
CALORIES: 130 per 4-oz. serving

· · · · · ·

ingredients

2¾ cups almond milk, divided

1 package (3.4 ounces) butterscotch instant pudding mix

½ cup (2 ounces) walnuts, toasted

1 cup (2 ounces) mini marshmallows, frozen

· · · · · ·

mix-in options

**BUTTERSCOTCH CHIPS
CARAMEL SAUCE
CARAMEL SQUARES**

method

1. In a large mixing bowl, pour 2 cups of almond milk. Add the butterscotch pudding mix into the almond milk. Lightly whisk the mixture using a wire whisk until dissolved, approximately one minute. Do not overmix or the mixture will thicken and not be easy to pour.

2. Pour the mixture into two standard ice cube trays, equally distributing between the two.

3. Place the ice cube trays in the freezer and freeze for eight hours or overnight.

4. In a Ninja 56-ounce food-processing bowl fitted with the standard blade attachment, place all the frozen butterscotch ice cubes. Add the remaining ¾ cup of almond milk. Using the crush function, process for 25 seconds.

5. Remove the lid and add the walnuts and mini marshmallows. Place the lid back on the food-processing bowl and crush for 13 seconds.

6. Remove the lid, carefully remove the blades, and serve.

T he lime zest with the lemon gives this ice cream a real key lime flavor. The graham crackers add the crunch that makes you sure you are eating ice-cold key lime pie.

key lime lemon pie ice cream

YIELD: 1¼ pints
SERVES: 6
PREP TIME: 12 minutes
CALORIES: 125 per 4-oz. serving

· · · · ·

ingredients

**2½ cups plus
1 tablespoon vanilla-
flavored soy milk,
divided**

**1 package (3.4 ounces)
lemon instant
pudding mix**

3 tablespoons lime zest

**1 tablespoon
granulated sugar**

**1 ounce graham
crackers, broken
into pieces**

· · · · ·

mix-in options

**CRUSHED LEMON
DROPS
FROZEN PIE CRUST
LEMON ZEST**

method

1. In a large mixing bowl, pour 2 cups of vanilla-flavored soy milk. Add the lemon pudding mix into the soy milk. Lightly whisk the mixture using a wire whisk until dissolved, approximately one minute. Do not overmix or the mixture will thicken and not be easy to pour.

2. Pour the mixture into two standard ice cube trays, equally distributing between the two.

3. Place the ice cube trays in the freezer and freeze for eight hours or overnight.

4. In a Ninja 56-ounce food-processing bowl fitted with the standard blade attachment, place half of the frozen lemon ice cubes. Evenly distribute the lime zest throughout and then add the remaining half of the frozen lemon ice cubes. Mix the remaining ½ cup and 1 tablespoon of vanilla-flavored soy milk with the sugar. Pour mixture into the food-processing bowl. Using the crush function, process for 20 seconds.

5. Remove the lid and add the graham crackers. Place the lid back on the food-processing bowl and crush for 13 seconds.

6. Remove the lid, carefully remove the blades, and serve.

I *f you like coconut, almonds, and fudge, this may become your favorite!*

coconut almond ice cream

YIELD: 1½ pints
SERVES: 6
PREP TIME: 9 minutes
CALORIES: 160 per 4-oz. serving

· · · · · ·

ingredients

2¾ cups coconut milk beverage, divided

1 package (3.4 ounces) coconut cream instant pudding mix

2½ ounces roasted almonds

2 ounces fudge, frozen and cut into ½-inch pieces

· · · · · ·

mix-in options

**CHOCOLATE CHUNKS
TOASTED COCONUT
CARAMEL SAUCE**

method

1. In a large mixing bowl, pour 2 cups of coconut milk beverage. Add the coconut cream pudding mix into the coconut milk beverage. Lightly whisk the mixture using a wire whisk until dissolved, approximately one minute. Do not overmix or the mixture will thicken and not be easy to pour.

2. Pour the mixture into two standard ice cube trays, equally distributing between the two.

3. Place the ice cube trays in the freezer and freeze for eight hours or overnight.

4. In a Ninja 56-ounce food-processing bowl fitted with the standard blade attachment, place all the frozen coconut cream ice cubes. Add the remaining ¾ cup of coconut milk beverage, roasted almonds, and fudge. Using the crush function, process for 50 seconds.

5. Remove the lid, carefully remove the blades, and serve.

This combination of rice pudding flavor, pistachios, and cherries for crunch is both flavorful and fulfilling.

pistachio rice pudding ice cream

YIELD: 1½ pints
SERVES: 6
PREP TIME: 10 minutes
CALORIES: 121 per 4-oz. serving

. . . . . .

ingredients

2 cups skim milk

1 package (3.4 ounces) pistachio instant pudding mix

1 cup (8 ounces) pre-made rice pudding

½ teaspoon ground cinnamon

½ cup (3 ounces) dried cherries

. . . . . .

mix-in options

**PISTACHIOS
NUTMEG
PINE NUTS**

method

1. In a large mixing bowl, pour the skim milk. Add the pistachio pudding mix into the skim milk. Lightly whisk the mixture using a wire whisk until dissolved, approximately one minute. Do not overmix or the mixture will thicken and not be easy to pour.

2. Pour the mixture into two standard ice cube trays, equally distributing between the two.

3. Place the ice cube trays in the freezer and freeze for eight hours or overnight.

4. In a Ninja 56-ounce food-processing bowl fitted with the standard blade attachment, place all the frozen pistachio ice cubes. Add the premade rice pudding, ground cinnamon, and dried cherries. Using the crush function, process for 50 seconds.

5. Remove the lid, carefully remove the blades, and serve.

E*veryone likes cookies, cheesecake, and chocolate. This is one decadent ice cream!*

cookies & cream chocolate cheesecake ice cream

YIELD: 1½ pints
SERVES: 6
PREP TIME: 15 minutes
CALORIES: 257 per 4-oz. serving

• • • • • •

ingredients

2 cups skim milk

**1 package (3.4 ounces)
cheesecake instant
pudding mix**

**4 ounces cream
cheese, cut into
½-inch pieces**

**⅓ cup plus
1 tablespoon hot
fudge sauce**

**3¼ ounces cream-
filled chocolate
sandwich cookies**

• • • • • •

mix-in options

**FROZEN
STRAWBERRIES
FROZEN RASPBERIES
CHOCOLATE CHIPS**

method

1. In a large mixing bowl, pour the skim milk. Add the cheesecake pudding mix into the skim milk. Lightly whisk the mixture using a wire whisk until dissolved, approximately one minute. Do not overmix or the mixture will thicken and not be easy to pour.

2. Pour the mixture into two standard ice cube trays, equally distributing between the two.

3. Place the ice cube trays in the freezer and freeze for eight hours or overnight.

4. In a Ninja 56-ounce food-processing bowl fitted with the standard blade attachment, place half the frozen cheesecake ice cubes, then add the cream cheese and hot fudge sauce. Add the other half of the frozen cheesecake ice cubes. Using the crush function, process for 35 seconds.

5. Remove the lid and add the cream-filled chocolate sandwich cookies. Place the lid back on the food-processing bowl and crush for 15 seconds.

6. Remove the lid, carefully remove the blades, and serve.

T his is a specialty item, as you do have to purchase a frozen tiramisu at your local grocery, but it is well worth the effort.

tiramisu ice cream

YIELD: 1½ pints
SERVES: 6
PREP TIME: 15 minutes
CALORIES: 172 per 4-oz. serving

· · · · · ·

ingredients

2 cups skim milk

1 package (3.4 ounces) vanilla instant pudding mix

8 ounces tiramisu, frozen and cut into 1-inch pieces

4 ounces coffee, room temperature

1 ounce dark chocolate chips

· · · · · ·

mix-in options

**CHOCOLATE SYRUP
COFFEE BEANS
ICE CREAM CONES**

method

1. In a large mixing bowl, pour the skim milk. Add the vanilla pudding mix into the skim milk. Lightly whisk the mixture using a wire whisk until dissolved, approximately one minute. Do not overmix or the mixture will thicken and not be easy to pour.

2. Pour the mixture into two standard ice cube trays, equally distributing between the two.

3. Place the ice cube trays in the freezer and freeze for eight hours or overnight.

4. In a Ninja 56-ounce food-processing bowl fitted with the standard blade attachment, place half the frozen vanilla ice cubes, then add the tiramisu and coffee. Add the other half of the frozen vanilla ice cubes. Using the crush function, process for 40 seconds.

5. Remove the lid and add the dark chocolate chips. Place the lid back on the food-processing bowl and crush for 20 seconds.

6. Remove the lid, carefully remove the blades, and serve.

C hocolate and orange are two of nature's natural flavor combinations that never fail to delight the palate.

chocolate orange ice cream

YIELD: 1½ pints
SERVES: 6
PREP TIME: 12 minutes
CALORIES: 168 per 4-oz. serving

· · · · · ·

ingredients

**2 cups plus
1 tablespoon vanilla-
flavored soy milk,
divided**

**1 package (3.56
ounces) white
chocolate instant
pudding mix**

**⅓ cup orange
marmalade**

**2 tablespoons
orange zest**

**⅓ cup semi-sweet mini
chocolate chips**

· · · · · ·

mix-in options

**WHITE CHOCOLATE
CHIPS
FROZEN MANDARIN
ORANGES
CHOCOLATE SAUCE**

method

1. In a large mixing bowl, pour 2 cups of vanilla-flavored soy milk. Add the white chocolate pudding mix into the soy milk. Lightly whisk the mixture using a wire whisk until dissolved, approximately one minute. Do not overmix or the mixture will thicken and not be easy to pour.

2. Pour the mixture into two standard ice cube trays, equally distributing between the two.

3. Place the ice cube trays in the freezer and freeze for eight hours or overnight.

4. In a Ninja 56-ounce food-processing bowl fitted with the standard blade attachment, place half of the frozen white chocolate ice cubes. Evenly distribute the orange marmalade and orange zest throughout, then add the remaining half of frozen white chocolate ice cubes. Add the remaining 1 tablespoon of vanilla-flavored soy milk. Using the crush function, process for 15 seconds.

5. Remove the lid and add the semi-sweet mini chocolate chips. Place the lid back on the food-processing bowl and crush for 15 seconds.

6. Remove the lid, carefully remove the blades, and serve.

P istachio is one of America's favorite flavors. This ice cream adds the pistachio crunch that makes it distinctive and delicious.

loaded pistachio ice cream

YIELD: 1½ pints
SERVES: 6
PREP TIME: 8 minutes
CALORIES: 236 per 4-oz. serving

· · · · ·

ingredients

**2½ cups plus
2 tablespoons whole
milk, divided**

**1 package (3.4 ounces)
pistachio instant
pudding mix**

**¾ cup (4 ounces)
pistachios, shelled**

· · · · ·

mix-in options

**CASHEWS
ICE CREAM CONE
RICE KRISPIES**

method

1. In a large mixing bowl, pour 2 cups of whole milk. Add the pistachio pudding mix into the milk. Lightly whisk the mixture using a wire whisk until dissolved, approximately one minute. Do not overmix or the mixture will thicken and not be easy to pour.

2. Pour the mixture into two standard ice cube trays, equally distributing between the two.

3. Place the ice cube trays in the freezer and freeze for eight hours or overnight.

4. In a Ninja 56-ounce food-processing bowl fitted with the standard blade attachment, place all the frozen pistachio ice cubes. Add the remaining ½ cup plus 2 tablespoons of whole milk. Using the crush function, process for 45 seconds.

5. Remove the lid and add the pistachios. Place the lid back on the food-processing bowl and crush for 15 seconds.

6. Remove the lid, carefully remove the blades, and serve.

*O*ur intern from the Hun School in Princeton came up with this recipe. She named it after her school, where she just graduated and is now headed to the Univeristy of Michigan to study engineering. Her plans are to be a food scientist. If this recipe is any indication, she has the natural talent to be a great recipe developer.

a hun-ny of a coffee ice cream

YIELD: 2 pints
SERVES: 8
PREP TIME: 15 minutes
CALORIES: 256 per 4-oz. serving

. . . . . .

ingredients

2 cups whole milk plus 2 tablespoons, divided

1 package (3.4 ounces) vanilla pudding mix

½ cup espresso coffee, cold from instant

¼ cup half-and-half

½ cup dark-chocolate-covered almonds

. . . . . .

mix-in options

MARSHMALLOWS
CHOCOLATE CHUNKS
CARAMEL BITS

method

1. In a large mixing bowl, pour 2 cups of whole milk. Add the vanilla pudding mix into the whole milk. Lightly whisk the mixture using a wire whisk until dissolved, approximately one minute. Do not overmix or the mixture will thicken and not be easy to pour.

2. Pour the mixture into two standard ice cube trays, equally distributing between the two.

3. Place the ice cube trays in the freezer and freeze for eight hours or overnight.

4. In a Ninja 56-ounce food-processing bowl fitted with the standard blade attachment, place all the frozen vanilla ice cubes. Add ½ cup of cold espresso coffee, plus the half-and-half. Using the crush function, process for 30 seconds.

5. Remove the lid and add the dark-chocolate-covered almonds. Place the lid back on the food-processing bowl and crush for 30 seconds.

6. Remove the lid, carefully remove the blades, and serve.

Strawberry Ice Cream, 78

fruit-based ice cream

paradise punch ice cream 71

peach ice cream 73

peachy cheesecake ice cream. 74

tropical burst ice cream 75

pineapple caramel ice cream 76

chocolate-coated cherry ice cream 77

strawberry ice cream 78

blueberry rice pudding ice cream 79

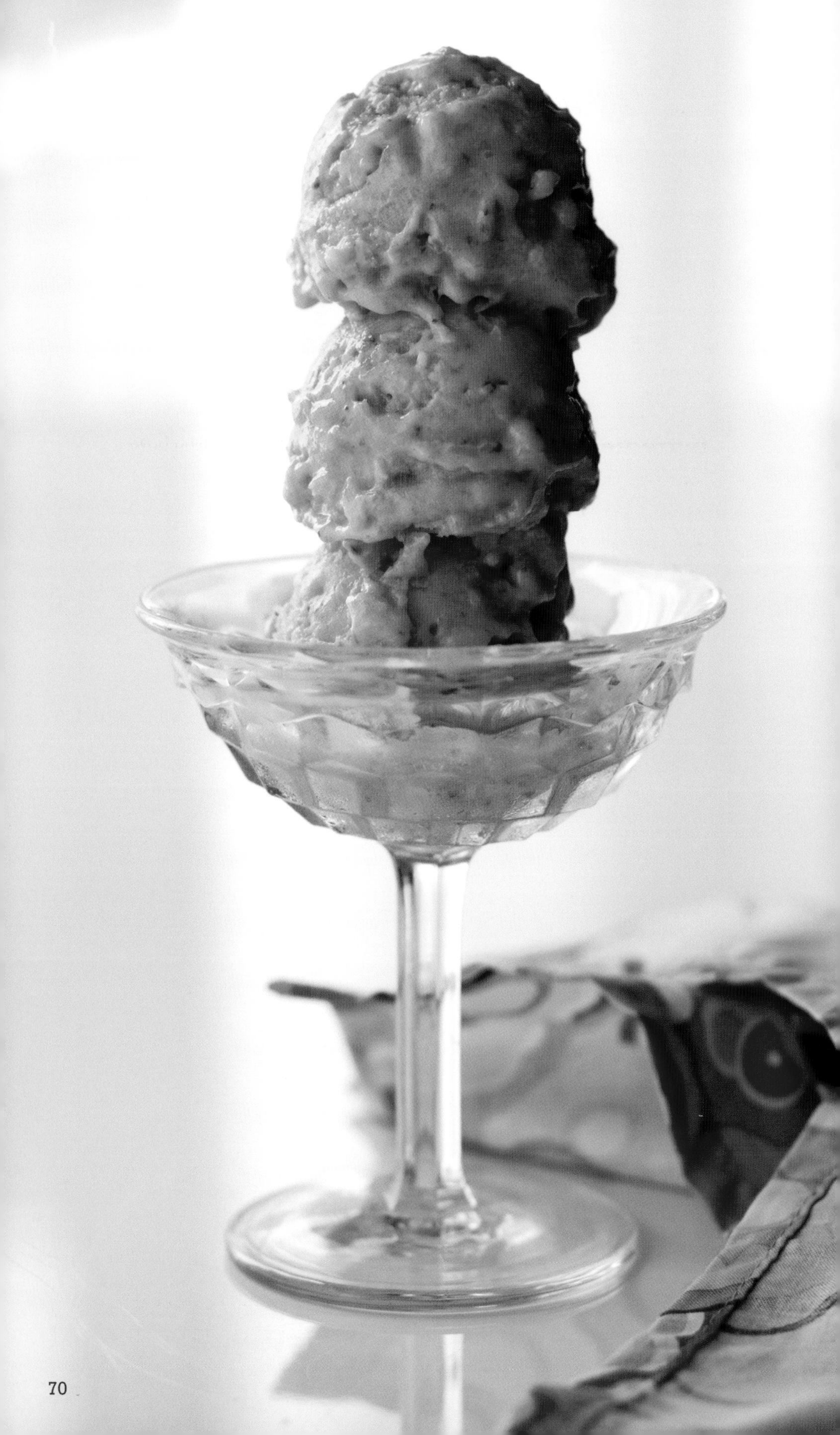

T his combination of frozen fruit makes a delicious low-calorie ice cream that you can make as often as you want and feel good about eating ice cream.

paradise punch ice cream

YIELD: 2¾ cups
SERVES: 6
PREP TIME: 2 minutes
CALORIES: 80 per 4-oz. serving

• • • • •

ingredients

1 cup whole milk

3 tablespoons sugar

1 pound frozen fruit medley chunks (peaches, strawberries, mangoes, and pineapple)

• • • • •

method

1. In a small mixing bowl, pour the whole milk. Add the sugar and mix until dissolved.

2. In a Ninja 56-ounce food-processing bowl fitted with the standard blade attachment, place the frozen fruit medley chunks. Add the whole milk and sugar mixture. Using the crush function, process for 35 seconds.

3. Remove the lid, carefully remove the blades, and serve.

T *his ice cream was the most searched for Ninja ice cream for the last four years. It is only 81 calories and is delicious.*

peach ice cream

YIELD: 1½ pints
SERVES: 6
PREP TIME: 3 minutes
CALORIES: 81 per 4-oz. serving

· · · · ·

ingredients

1 pound frozen peach slices

⅓ cup sugar substitute

1 cup plus 2 tablespoons skim milk

· · · · ·

method

1. In a Ninja 56-ounce food-processing bowl fitted with the standard blade attachment, place the frozen peach slices. Dissolve the sugar substitute in the skim milk, then add to food-processing bowl. Using the crush function, process for 40 seconds.

2. Remove the lid, carefully remove the blades, and serve.

I f you have leftover cheesecake, freeze it! Then you can make this ice cream when you are ready for an unbelievable treat.

peachy cheesecake ice cream

YIELD: 2¾ cups
SERVES: 6
PREP TIME: 4 minutes
CALORIES: 289 per 4-oz. serving

• • • • •

ingredients

8 ounces frozen peach slices

8 ounces cheesecake, frozen, cut into 1-inch pieces

⅔ cup heavy cream

• • • • •

method

1. In a Ninja 56-ounce food-processing bowl fitted with the standard blade attachment, place the frozen peach slices and the frozen cheesecake pieces. Add the heavy cream. Using the crush function, process for 35 seconds.

2. Remove the lid, carefully remove the blades, and serve.

I f you are ever going to have ice cream for breakfast, this is the one.

tropical burst
ice cream

YIELD: 3 cups
SERVES: 6
PREP TIME: 3 minutes
CALORIES: 95 per 6-oz. serving

• • • • •

ingredients

**12 ounces frozen
mango chunks**

**4 ounces frozen
pineapple chunks**

**1 cup canned lite
coconut milk**

**¼ cup tropical-fruit-
flavored coconut water**

• • • • •

method

1. In a Ninja 56-ounce food-processing bowl fitted with the standard blade attachment, place the frozen mango and pineapple chunks. Add the light coconut milk and tropical-fruit-flavored coconut water. Using the crush function, process for 25 seconds.

2. Remove the lid, carefully remove the blades, and serve.

Pineapple and caramel! Who would have thought that this would make such a delightful combination?

pineapple caramel ice cream

YIELD: 2½ cups
SERVES: 6
PREP TIME: 4 minutes
CALORIES: 150 per 4-oz. serving

• • • • •

ingredients

1 pound frozen pineapple chunks

¼ cup half-and-half

⅓ cup plus 2 tablespoons caramel sauce

• • • • •

method

1. In a Ninja 56-ounce food-processing bowl fitted with the standard blade attachment, place the frozen pineapple chunks. Add the half-and-half and caramel sauce. Using the crush function, process for 30 seconds.

2. Remove the lid, carefully remove the blades, and serve.

Y ou won't believe how well the cherries and strawberries
dance together in this tongue-tingling recipe!

chocolate-coated cherry ice cream

YIELD: 2¾ cups
SERVES: 6
PREP TIME: 10 minutes
CALORIES: 157 per 4-oz. serving

· · · · ·

ingredients

10 ounces frozen dark sweet cherries

8 ounces whole frozen strawberries

⅓ cup soy milk

¼ cup chocolate syrup

⅓ cup (2 ounces) mini semi-sweet chocolate chips

· · · · ·

method

1. In a Ninja 56-ounce food-processing bowl fitted with the standard blade attachment, place the frozen cherries and strawberries. Add the soy milk and chocolate syrup. Using the crush function, process for 25 seconds.

2. Remove the lid and add the mini semi-sweet chocolate chips. Place the lid back on the food-processing bowl and crush for 10 seconds.

3. Remove the lid, carefully remove the blades, and serve.

This recipe tastes like summer! When in season, pick your strawberries fresh and freeze them so that during the cold months, you can warm up your heart.

strawberry ice cream

YIELD: 3 cups
SERVES: 6
PREP TIME: 4 minutes
CALORIES: 126 per 4-oz. serving

. . . . .

ingredients

1 pound whole frozen strawberries

½ cup half-and-half

½ cup low-sugar strawberry preserves

. . . . .

method

1. In a Ninja 56-ounce food-processing bowl fitted with the standard blade attachment, place the frozen strawberries. Add the half-and-half and strawberry preserves. Using the crush function, process for 30 seconds.

2. Remove the lid, carefully remove the blades, and serve.

*I*f you like rice pudding and blueberries, this is the ice cream you have been waiting to taste. It could become your favorite.

blueberry rice pudding ice cream

YIELD: 3 cups
SERVES: 6
PREP TIME: 3 minutes
CALORIES: 88 per 4-oz. serving

· · · · ·

ingredients

1 pound frozen blueberries

½ teaspoon ground cinnamon

1 cup premade original-flavor rice pudding

· · · · ·

method

1. In a Ninja 56-ounce food-processing bowl fitted with the standard blade attachment, place the frozen blueberries. Sprinkle the cinnamon on top of the frozen blueberries. Add the rice pudding. Using the crush function, process for 30 seconds.

2. Remove the lid, carefully remove the blades, and serve.

**Blueberry Rice Pudding
Ice Cream, 79**

low-calorie d'lites

banana maple ice cream 83

café mocha chip ice cream 85

lemon gingersnap bar ice cream 87

mixed-berry smoothie ice cream 89

raspberry rush sorbet 91

snickerdoodle cookie ice cream 93

cherries jubilee ice cream 94

chocolate candy ice cream 95

italian cookie ice cream 96

my favorite frozen yogurt 97

T his low-calorie, low-fat recipe is delicious. For a more decadent ice cream, you can substitute whole milk or heavy cream for the soy milk.

banana maple ice cream

YIELD: 1½ pints
SERVES: 6
PREP TIME: 8 minutes
CALORIES: 95 per 4-oz. serving

· · · · ·

ingredients

**2 cups plus
3 tablespoons vanilla-
flavored soy milk,
divided**

**1 package (3.4 ounces)
sugar-free banana
cream instant
pudding mix**

**1 banana, peeled, cut
into 1-inch pieces**

**½ teaspoon ground
cinnamon**

¼ cup maple syrup

· · · · ·

method

1. In a large mixing bowl, pour 2 cups of vanilla-flavored soy milk. Add the banana pudding mix into the soy milk. Lightly whisk the mixture using a wire whisk until dissolved, approximately one minute. Do not overmix or the mixture will thicken and not be easy to pour.

2. Pour the mixture into two standard ice cube trays, equally distributing between the two.

3. Place the ice cube trays in the freezer and freeze for eight hours or overnight.

4. In a Ninja 56-ounce food-processing bowl fitted with the standard blade attachment, place all the frozen banana ice cubes. Add the remaining 3 tablespoons of vanilla-flavored soy milk, banana, ground cinnamon, and maple syrup. Using the crush function, process for 30 seconds.

5. Remove the lid, carefully remove the blades, and serve.

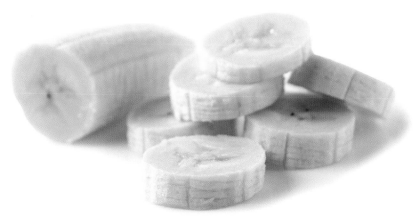

E specially for coffee lovers, this ice cream is a real pick-me-up!

café mocha chip ice cream

YIELD: 1½ pints
SERVES: 6
PREP TIME: 13 minutes
CALORIES: 96 per 4-oz. serving

• • • • • •

ingredients

2 cups whole milk

1 package (3.56 ounces) white chocolate instant pudding mix

⅓ cup espresso, room temperature

¼ cup chocolate-covered espresso beans

• • • • • •

method

1. In a large mixing bowl, pour the whole milk. Add the white chocolate pudding mix into the milk. Lightly whisk the mixture using a wire whisk until dissolved, approximately one minute. Do not overmix or the mixture will thicken and not be easy to pour.

2. Pour the mixture into two standard ice cube trays, equally distributing between the two.

3. Place the ice cube trays in the freezer and freeze for eight hours or overnight.

4. In a Ninja 56-ounce food-processing bowl fitted with the standard blade attachment, place all the frozen white chocolate ice cubes. Add the espresso. Using the crush function, process for 30 seconds.

5. Remove the lid and add the chocolate-covered espresso beans. Place the lid back on the food-processing bowl and crush for 12 seconds.

6. Remove the lid, carefully remove the blades, and serve.

F*ewer than 100 calories per serving. Crunchy, lemony, and delicious!*

lemon gingersnap bar ice cream

YIELD: 1½ pints
SERVES: 6
PREP TIME: 8 minutes
CALORIES: 100 per 4-oz. serving

· · · · ·

ingredients

2⅔ cups skim milk, divided

1 package (3.4 ounces) lemon instant pudding mix

2¼ ounces gingersnap cookies, broken in half

· · · · ·

method

1. In a large mixing bowl, pour 2 cups of skim milk. Add the lemon pudding mix into the skim milk. Lightly whisk the mixture using a wire whisk until dissolved, approximately one minute. Do not overmix or the mixture will thicken and not be easy to pour.

2. Pour the mixture into two standard ice cube trays, equally distributing between the two.

3. Place the ice cube trays in the freezer and freeze for eight hours or overnight.

4. In a Ninja 56-ounce food-processing bowl fitted with the standard blade attachment, place all the frozen lemon ice cubes. Add the remaining ⅔ cup of skim milk. Using the crush function, process for 30 seconds.

5. Remove the lid and add the gingersnap cookies. Place the lid back on the food-processing bowl and crush for 25 seconds.

6. Remove the lid, carefully remove the blades, and serve.

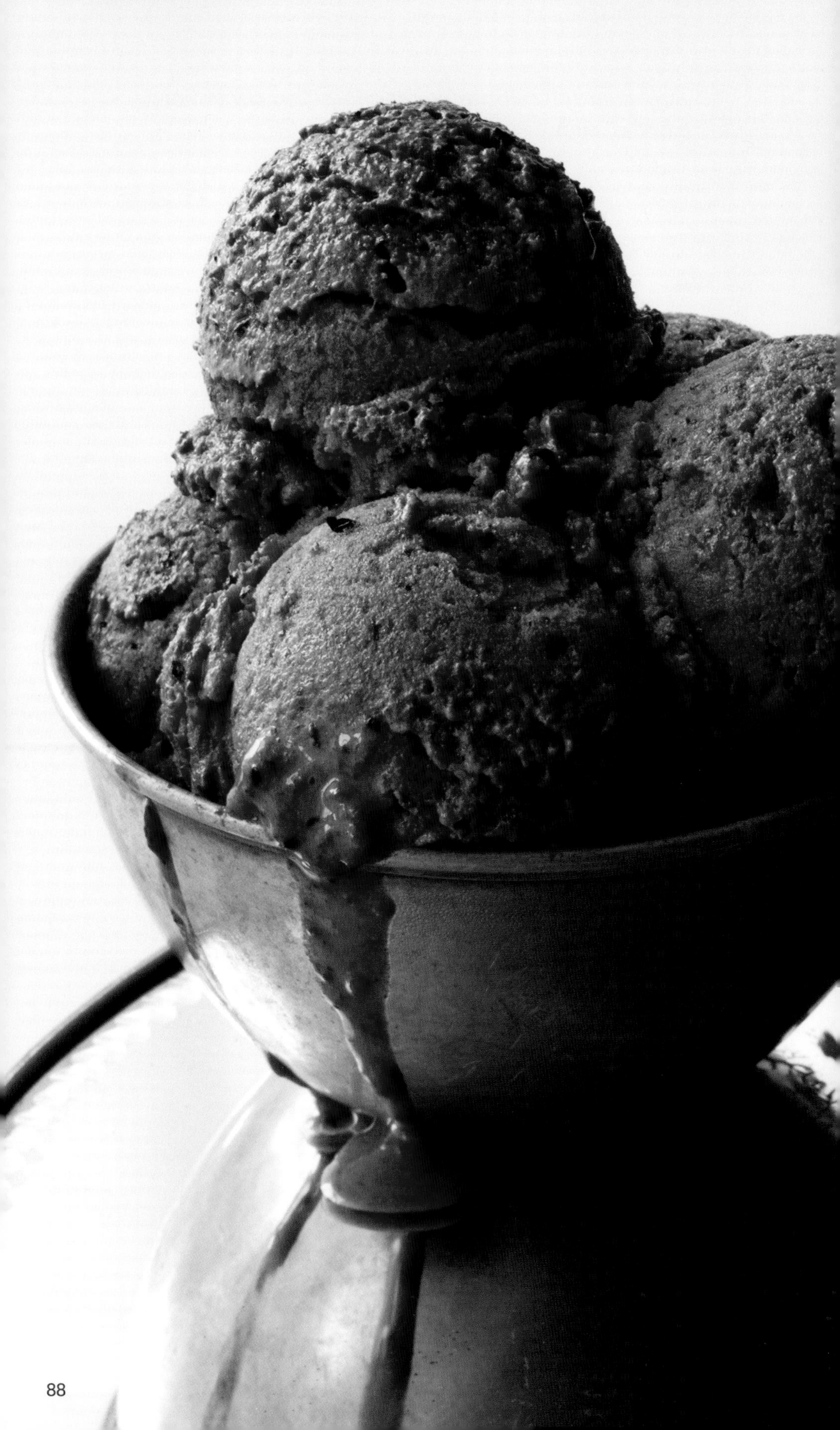

*A*nother favorite of our ice-cream-tasting panel. This recipe really pops in your mouth, and you can eat a double portion and still be under 100 calories!

mixed-berry smoothie ice cream

YIELD: 3 cups
SERVES: 6
PREP TIME: 2 minutes
CALORIES: 38 per 4-oz. serving

• • • • •

ingredients

1⅛ cups plain low-fat liquid yogurt beverage or plain low-fat cultured-milk smoothie beverage

3 tablespoons sugar substitute

1 pound frozen mixed berries (strawberries, blueberries, blackberries, and raspberries)

• • • • •

method

1. In a small mixing bowl, pour the liquid yogurt beverage or cultured-milk smoothie beverage. Add the sugar substitute and mix until dissolved.

2. In a Ninja 56-ounce food-processing bowl fitted with the standard blade attachment, place the frozen mixed berries. Add the liquid yogurt beverage or cultured-milk smoothie beverage and sugar mixture. Using the crush function, process for 30 seconds.

3. Remove the lid, carefully remove the blades, and serve.

Just 60 calories of pure raspberry and pear flavor. Create your own flavor by adding your favorite nectar instead of using pear.

raspberry rush sorbet

YIELD: 2½ cups
SERVES: 6
PREP TIME: 6 minutes
CALORIES: 60 per 4-oz. serving

· · · · · ·

ingredients

8 ounces pear nectar

1 tablespoon granulated sugar

1 pound frozen raspberries

1 pear, peeled, cored, cut into quarters

· · · · · ·

method

1. In a small mixing bowl, pour pear nectar. Add the sugar and mix until dissolved. Do not overmix or the mixture will thicken and will not be easy to pour.

2. In a Ninja 56-ounce food-processing bowl fitted with the standard blade attachment, place the frozen raspberries and quartered pear. Add the pear nectar and sugar mixture. Using the crush function, process for 35 seconds.

3. Remove the lid, carefully remove the blades, and serve.

T his ice cream has a real gelato feel that tastes fresh after every spoonful.

snickerdoodle cookie ice cream

YIELD: 1½ pints
SERVES: 6
PREP TIME: 10 minutes
CALORIES: 86 per 4-oz. serving

• • • • • •

ingredients

2⅔ cups whole milk, divided

1 package (3.56 ounces) white chocolate instant pudding mix

½ teaspoon ground cinnamon

¼ teaspoon nutmeg

1 tablespoon vanilla extract

• • • • • •

method

1. In a large mixing bowl, pour 2 cups of whole milk. Add the white chocolate pudding mix into the milk. Lightly whisk the mixture using a wire whisk until dissolved, approximately one minute. Do not overmix or the mixture will thicken and not be easy to pour.

2. Pour the mixture into two standard ice cube trays, equally distributing between the two.

3. Place the ice cube trays in the freezer and freeze for eight hours or overnight.

4. In a Ninja 56-ounce food-processing bowl fitted with the standard blade attachment, place all the frozen white chocolate ice cubes. Add the remaining ⅔ cup of whole milk, cinnamon, nutmeg, and vanilla extract. Using the crush function, process for 45 seconds.

5. Remove the lid, carefully remove the blades, and serve.

Use the Ninja food processor to process the cherries into the bite size you want. Big chunks or little chunks — it's up to you.

cherries jubilee ice cream

YIELD: 1¾ pints
SERVES: 6
PREP TIME: 9 minutes
CALORIES: 62 per 4-oz. serving

· · · · · ·

ingredients

2⅓ cups almond milk, divided

1 package (3.4 ounces) French vanilla instant pudding mix

6 ounces frozen cherries

1 ounce cognac

· · · · · ·

method

1. In a large mixing bowl, pour 2 cups of almond milk. Add the French vanilla pudding mix into the almond milk. Lightly whisk the mixture using a wire whisk until dissolved, approximately one minute. Do not overmix or the mixture will thicken and not be easy to pour.

2. Pour the mixture into two standard ice cube trays, equally distributing between the two.

3. Place the ice cube trays in the freezer and freeze for eight hours or overnight.

4. In a Ninja 56-ounce food-processing bowl fitted with the standard blade attachment, place half of the frozen French vanilla ice cubes. Evenly distribute the frozen cherries throughout and then add the remaining half of frozen French vanilla ice cubes. Add the cognac. Using the crush function, process for 40 seconds.

5. Remove the lid, carefully remove the blades, and serve.

This is an all-time kids' favorite. How can you beat chocolate ice cream combined with your favorite candy-coated chocolate? This ice cream is perfect as a birthday party treat.

chocolate candy ice cream

YIELD: 1½ pints
SERVES: 6
PREP TIME: 8 minutes
CALORIES: 70 per 4-oz. serving

· · · · · ·

ingredients

2⅔ cups skim milk, divided

1 package (3.9 ounces) chocolate fudge instant pudding mix

½ cup (3½ ounces) candy-coated milk chocolate

· · · · · ·

method

1. In a large mixing bowl, pour 2 cups of skim milk. Add the chocolate fudge pudding mix into the skim milk. Lightly whisk the mixture using a wire whisk until dissolved, approximately one minute. Do not overmix or the mixture will thicken and not be easy to pour.

2. Pour the mixture into two standard ice cube trays, equally distributing between the two.

3. Place the ice cube trays in the freezer and freeze for eight hours or overnight.

4. In a Ninja 56-ounce food-processing bowl fitted with the standard blade attachment, place all the frozen chocolate fudge ice cubes. Add the remaining ⅔ cup of skim milk. Using the crush function, process for 35 seconds.

5. Remove the lid and add the candy-coated milk chocolate. Place the lid back on the food-processing bowl and crush for 20 seconds.

6. Remove the lid, carefully remove the blades, and serve.

W*hite chocolate has its own distinct flavor. Almond milk makes the perfect base for this crunchy biscotti ice cream.*

italian cookie ice cream

YIELD: 1¼ cups
SERVES: 6
PREP TIME: 8 minutes
CALORIES: 76 per 4-oz. serving

• • • • •

ingredients

2¾ cups almond milk, divided

1 package (3.56 ounces) white chocolate instant pudding mix

½ teaspoon almond extract

2 ounces almond-flavored biscotti, broken into pieces

• • • • •

method

1. In a large mixing bowl, pour 2 cups of almond milk. Add the white chocolate pudding mix into the almond milk. Lightly whisk the mixture using a wire whisk until dissolved, approximately one minute. Do not overmix or the mixture will thicken and not be easy to pour.

2. Pour the mixture into two standard ice cube trays, equally distributing between the two.

3. Place the ice cube trays in the freezer and freeze for eight hours or overnight.

4. In a Ninja 56-ounce food-processing bowl fitted with the standard blade attachment, place all the frozen white chocolate ice cubes. Add the remaining ¾ cup of almond milk and the almond extract. Using the crush function, process for 25 seconds.

5. Remove the lid and add the biscotti. Place the lid back on the food-processing bowl and crush for 20 seconds.

6. Remove the lid, carefully remove the blades, and serve.

This is a great fruit and yogurt ice cream. It is the lowest-calorie ice cream in this book!

my favorite frozen yogurt

YIELD: 3 cups
SERVES: 6
PREP TIME: 2 minutes
CALORIES: 37 per 4-oz. serving

· · · · ·

ingredients

1 cup plus 3 tablespoons plain low-fat liquid yogurt beverage or plain low-fat cultured-milk smoothie beverage

2 tablespoons sugar substitute

1 pound frozen tropical fruit medley chunks (kiwis, strawberries, papaya, mangoes and pineapple)

· · · · ·

method

1. In a small mixing bowl, pour in the liquid yogurt beverage or cultured-milk smoothie beverage. Add the sugar substitute and mix until dissolved.

2. In a Ninja 56-ounce food-processing bowl fitted with the standard blade attachment, place the frozen tropical fruit medley chunks. Add the liquid yogurt beverage or cultured-milk smoothie beverage and sugar mixture. Using the crush function, process for 35 seconds.

3. Remove the lid, carefully remove the blades, and serve.

Malted Milkshake, 109

milkshakes & coffee drinks

mint cookies & cream milkshake..........................101

caramel éclair milkshake................................103

cherry cheesecake milkshake............................105

mocha chocolate milkshake..............................107

pumpkin coffee milkshake...............................108

malted milkshake......................................109

bananas foster milkshake...............................110

pistachio rocky road milkshake.........................111

boston cream pie milkshake.............................112

peanut butter cookie milkshake.........................113

strawberry milkshake..................................114

marshmallow crème milkshake..........................115

chocolate coconut iced-coffee milkshake.................118

dulce de leche coffee drink.............................116

raspberry coffee milkshake.............................117

hazelnut chocolate coffee soy milkshake................119

T*his is one of the most delicious minty, chocolate-flavored shakes ever!*

mint cookies & cream milkshake

YIELD: 9 cups (72 oz.)
SERVES: 6
PREP TIME: 12 minutes
CALORIES: 339 per 12-oz. serving

· · · · ·

ingredients

5¼ cups whole milk, divided

1 package (3.9 ounces) chocolate fudge instant pudding mix

6 ounces peppermint patties

4 ounces cream-filled chocolate sandwich cookies

· · · · ·

mix-in options

CRUSHED CANDY BARS

method

1. In a large mixing bowl, pour 2 cups of whole milk. Add the chocolate fudge pudding mix into the milk. Lightly whisk the mixture using a wire whisk until dissolved, approximately one minute. Do not overmix or the mixture will thicken and not be easy to pour.

2. Pour the mixture into two standard ice cube trays, equally distributing between the two.

3. Place the ice cube trays in the freezer and freeze for eight hours or overnight.

For 72-Ounce Blender:

4. In a Ninja 72-ounce pitcher fitted with the standard blade attachment, place all the frozen chocolate fudge ice cubes. Add the remaining 3¼ cups of whole milk, peppermint patties, and cream-filled chocolate sandwich cookies. Using the crush function, process for 50 seconds.

5. Remove the lid, carefully remove the blades, and serve.

For Single-Serve Cup:

1. In a Ninja 16-ounce single-serve cup, place 5 ounces of chocolate fudge ice cubes. Add 1½ ounces of peppermint patties, cut in half; 1¼ ounces cream-filled chocolate sandwich cookies; and 1 cup of whole milk. Put bladed lid onto cup and blend on single-serve setting for 25 seconds. Carefully remove blades, put on drinking lid, and enjoy.

W e d'éclair this to be delicious—classic custard flavors made into a milkshake.

caramel éclair milkshake

YIELD: 7 cups (56 oz.)
SERVES: 6
PREP TIME: 10 minutes
CALORIES: 360 per 9-oz. serving

. . . . . .

ingredients

4½ cups whole milk, divided

1 package (3.4 ounces) vanilla instant pudding mix

¾ cup caramel sauce

6 ounces mini cream puffs, frozen

. . . . . .

mix-in options

CRUSHED CANDY BARS

method

1. In a large mixing bowl, pour 2 cups of whole milk. Add the vanilla pudding mix into the milk. Lightly whisk the mixture using a wire whisk until dissolved, approximately one minute. Do not overmix or the mixture will thicken and not be easy to pour.

2. Pour the mixture into two standard ice cube trays, equally distributing between the two.

3. Place the ice cube trays in the freezer and freeze for eight hours or overnight.

For 72-Ounce Blender:

4. In a Ninja 72-ounce pitcher fitted with the standard blade attachment, place all the frozen vanilla ice cubes. Add the remaining 2½ cups of whole milk, caramel sauce, and mini cream puffs. Using the crush function, process for 35 seconds.

5. Remove the lid, carefully remove the blades, and serve.

For Single-Serve Cup:

1. In a Ninja 16-ounce single-serve cup, place 6 ounces of vanilla ice cubes. Add 3 tablespoons of caramel sauce, 1½ ounces of frozen mini cream puffs, and 1 cup of whole milk. Put bladed lid onto cup and blend on single-serve setting for 20 seconds. Carefully remove blades, put on drinking lid, and enjoy.

I f you love cherry cheesecake, you will really enjoy this milkshake. The graham crackers add just the right taste to this faux cheesecake.

cherry cheesecake milkshake

YIELD: 8½ cups (68 oz.)
SERVES: 6
PREP TIME: 12 minutes
CALORIES: 266 per 11-oz. serving

. . . . .

ingredients

5 cups whole milk, divided

1 package (3.4 ounces) cheesecake instant pudding mix

6 ounces cheesecake, frozen, cut into 1-inch cubes

6 ounces frozen cherries

1 ounce graham crackers, broken into 1-inch pieces

. . . . .

mix-in options

FROZEN STRAWBERRIES
FROZEN RASPBERRIES
FROZEN BLUEBERRIESS

method

1. In a large mixing bowl, pour 2 cups of whole milk. Add the cheesecake pudding mix into the milk. Lightly whisk the mixture using a wire whisk until dissolved, approximately one minute. Do not overmix or the mixture will thicken and not be easy to pour.

2. Pour the mixture into two standard ice cube trays, equally distributing between the two.

3. Place the ice cube trays in the freezer and freeze for eight hours or overnight.

For 72-Ounce Blender:

4. In a Ninja 72-ounce pitcher fitted with the standard blade attachment, place all the frozen cheesecake ice cubes. Add the remaining 3 cups of whole milk, frozen cheesecake, frozen cherries, and graham crackers. Using the crush function, process for 45 seconds.

5. Remove the lid, carefully remove the blades, and serve.

For Single-Serve Cup:

1. In a Ninja 16-ounce single-serve cup, place 5 ounces of cheesecake ice cubes. Add 1 ounce of frozen cheesecake, cut into cubes; 1½ ounces of frozen cherries; ¼ ounce of graham crackers, broken into pieces; and 1 cup of whole milk. Put bladed lid onto cup and blend on single-serve setting for 25 seconds. Carefully remove blades, put on drinking lid, and enjoy.

This will equal any coffee drink you will find at the Lots of Bucks coffee shops! And you can create your own options. If you like more chocolate and less coffee flavor, substitute chocolate instant pudding for vanilla. For lower-calorie versions, you can substitute low-fat milk and sugar-free instant pudding.

mocha chocolate milkshake

YIELD: 6 cups (48 oz.)
SERVES: 4
PREP TIME: 10 minutes
CALORIES: 147 per 12-oz. serving

• • • • •

ingredients

3 cups whole milk, divided

2 cups dark roasted coffee, cold

1 package (3.4 ounces) vanilla instant pudding mix

¼ cup sugar-free chocolate syrup or ¼ cup cocoa powder

• • • • •

method

1. In a large mixing bowl, pour 2 cups of whole milk. Add the vanilla pudding mix into the milk. Lightly whisk the mixture using a wire whisk until dissolved, approximately one minute. Do not overmix or the mixture will thicken and not be easy to pour.

2. Pour the mixture into two standard ice cube trays, equally distributing between the two.

3. Place the ice cube trays in the freezer and freeze for eight hours or overnight.

For 72-Ounce Blender:

4. In a Ninja 72-ounce pitcher fitted with the standard blade attachment, place all the frozen vanilla ice cubes. Add the remaining 1 cup of whole milk, cold coffee, and chocolate sauce or cocoa powder. Using the crush function, process approximately 35 seconds or until smooth.

5. Remove the lid, carefully remove the blades, and serve.

For Single-Serve Cup:

1. In a Ninja 16-ounce single-serve cup, place 5 ounces of vanilla ice cubes (¼ of total cubes). Add 4 ounces of cold coffee, 2 ounces of cold milk, and 1 tablespoon of chocolate syrup. Put bladed lid onto cup and blend on single-serve setting for 20 seconds. Carefully remove blades, put on drinking lid, and enjoy.

O n a cold day this cold pumpkin coffee shake is warm and comforting. Pumpkin mix, cinnamon, and nutmeg give this happy coffee drink its distinctly fall flavor.

pumpkin coffee milkshake

YIELD: 6 cups (48 oz.)
SERVES: 4
PREP TIME: 10 minutes
CALORIES: 109 per 12-oz. serving

· · · · ·

ingredients

2 cups low-fat milk

1 package (3.4 ounces) vanilla instant pudding mix

2 cups dark roasted coffee, cold

1 15-ounce can pumpkin puree

¼ cup brown sugar

1 teaspoon ground cinnamon

1 teaspoon ground nutmeg

· · · · ·

method

1. In a large mixing bowl, pour the low-fat milk. Add the vanilla pudding mix into the milk. Lightly whisk the mixture using a wire whisk until dissolved, approximately one minute. Do not overmix or the mixture will thicken and not be easy to pour.

2. Pour the mixture into two standard ice cube trays, equally distributing between the two.

3. Place the ice cube trays in the freezer and freeze for eight hours or overnight.

For 72-Ounce Blender:

4. In a Ninja 72-ounce pitcher fitted with the standard blade attachment, place all the frozen vanilla ice cubes. Add the pumpkin puree, cold coffee, brown sugar, cinnamon, and nutmeg. Using the crush function, process approximately 35 seconds or until smooth.

5. Remove the lid, carefully remove the blades, and serve.

For Single-Serve Cup:

1. In a Ninja 16-ounce single-serve cup, place 5 ounces of vanilla ice cubes (¼ of total cubes). Add 2 ounces of pumpkin puree, 4 ounces of cold coffee, ½ ounce brown sugar, ¼ teaspoon of ground cinnamon, and ¼ teaspoon ground nutmeg. Put bladed lid onto cup and blend on single-serve setting for 20 seconds. Carefully remove blades, put on drinking lid, and enjoy.

T*he easy-to-find malted milk balls give this shake an old-time richness and flavor from the 1960s.*

malted milkshake

YIELD: 8 cups (64 oz.)
SERVES: 6
PREP TIME: 10 minutes
CALORIES: 430 per 10-oz. serving

· · · · ·

ingredients

2½ cups whole milk

½ cup malted milk powder, original flavor

4 cups vanilla ice cream

1 tablespoon vanilla extract

3 ounces malted milk balls

· · · · ·

mix-in options

CHOCOLATE CHIPS
CHOCOLATE SYRUP

method

For 72-Ounce Blender:

1. In a small mixing bowl add 2½ cups of whole milk. Add ½ cup of malted milk powder. Stir until dissolved. Set aside.

2. In a Ninja 72-ounce pitcher fitted with the standard blade attachment, place the vanilla ice cream. Add the malted milk mixture, vanilla extract, and malted milk balls. Using the crush function, process for 30 seconds.

3. Remove the lid, carefully remove the blades, and serve.

For Single-Serve Cup:

1. In a Ninja 16-ounce single-serve cup, place ¾ ounce of malted milk balls, ¾ cup of whole milk, 2 tablespoons of malted milk powder, 1 cup of vanilla ice cream, and ½ teaspoon of vanilla extract. Put bladed lid onto cup and blend on single-serve setting for 25 seconds. Carefully remove blades, put on drinking lid, and enjoy.

*I*f you love bananas foster, you will love this delicious milkshake.

bananas foster milkshake

YIELD: 7 cups (56 oz.)
SERVES: 6
PREP TIME: 10 minutes
CALORIES: 162 per 9-oz. serving

· · · · ·

ingredients

4 cups whole milk, divided

1 package (3.4 ounces) butterscotch instant pudding mix

2 bananas, peeled

½ teaspoon ground cinnamon

3 tablespoons dark rum (optional)

· · · · ·

mix-in options

SPRINKLES
CRUSHED CANDY
BARS

method

1. In a large mixing bowl, pour 2 cups of whole milk. Add the butterscotch pudding mix into the milk. Lightly whisk the mixture using a wire whisk until dissolved, approximately one minute. Do not overmix or the mixture will thicken and not be easy to pour.

2. Pour the mixture into two standard ice cube trays, equally distributing between the two.

3. Place the ice cube trays in the freezer and freeze for eight hours or overnight.

For 72-Ounce Blender:

4. In a Ninja 72-ounce pitcher fitted with the standard blade attachment, place all the frozen butterscotch ice cubes. Add the remaining cups of whole milk, bananas, ground cinnamon, and the optional rum, if desired. Using the crush function, process for 30 seconds.

5. Remove the lid, carefully remove the blades, and serve.

For Single-Serve Cup:

1. In a Ninja 16-ounce single-serve cup, place 6 ounces of butterscotch ice cubes. Add ½ peeled banana, cut in half; ⅛ teaspoon of ground cinnamon, 2 teaspoons of dark rum, and 1 cup of whole milk. Put bladed lid onto cup and blend on single-serve setting for 20 seconds. Carefully remove blades, put on drinking lid, and enjoy.

T he almonds and marshmallows add the rocky road
deliciousness to this ice cream shake.

pistachio rocky road milkshake

YIELD: 7 cups (56 oz.)
SERVES: 6
PREP TIME: 10 minutes
CALORIES: 369 per 8-oz. serving

· · · · ·

ingredients

5 cups whole milk, divided

1 package (3.4 ounces) pistachio instant pudding mix

1 cup (2 ounces) mini marshmallows

½ cup (2½ ounces) roasted almonds

· · · · ·

mix-in options

PISTACHIOS
PEANUTS
PECANS

method

1. In a large mixing bowl, pour 2 cups of whole milk. Add the pistachio pudding mix into the milk. Lightly whisk the mixture using a wire whisk until dissolved, approximately one minute. Do not overmix or the mixture will thicken and not be easy to pour.

2. Pour the mixture into two standard ice cube trays, equally distributing between the two.

3. Place the ice cube trays in the freezer and freeze for eight hours or overnight.

For 72-Ounce Blender:

4. In a Ninja 72-ounce pitcher fitted with the standard blade attachment, place all the frozen pistachio ice cubes. Add the remaining 3 cups of whole milk, mini marshmallows, and roasted almonds. Using the crush function, process for one minute.

5. Remove the lid, carefully remove the blades, and serve.

For Single-Serve Cup:

1. In a Ninja 16-ounce single-serve cup, place 7 ounces of pistachio ice cubes. Add ½ ounce of mini marshmallows, 1 ounce of roasted almonds, and ¾ cup of whole milk. Put bladed lid onto cup and blend on single-serve setting for 25 seconds. Carefully remove blades, put on drinking lid, and enjoy.

T*his drink is a taste-great winner for sure. You may actually believe you are eating Boston cream pie.*

boston cream pie milkshake

YIELD: 7½ cups (58 oz.)
SERVES: 6
PREP TIME: 12 minutes
CALORIES: 275 per 9-oz. serving

· · · · ·

ingredients

5½ cups whole milk, divided

1 package (3.4 ounces) vanilla instant pudding mix

4 ounces all-butter pound cake, frozen, cut into 1-inch cubes

3 ounces chocolate fudge, frozen, cut into 1-inch cubes

· · · · ·

mix-in options

CHOCOLATE CHIPS
CHOCOLATE CHUNKS
GRAHAM CRACKERS

method

1. In a large mixing bowl, pour 2 cups of whole milk. Add the vanilla pudding mix into the milk. Lightly whisk the mixture using a wire whisk until dissolved, approximately one minute. Do not overmix or the mixture will thicken and not be easy to pour.

2. Pour the mixture into two standard ice cube trays, equally distributing between the two.

3. Place the ice cube trays in the freezer and freeze for eight hours or overnight.

For 72-Ounce Blender:

4. In a Ninja 72-ounce pitcher fitted with the standard blade attachment, place all the frozen vanilla ice cubes. Add the remaining 3½ cups of whole milk, all-butter pound cake and chocolate fudge. Using the crush function, process for 55 seconds.

5. Remove the lid, carefully remove the blades, and serve.

For Single-Serve Cup:

1. In a Ninja 16-ounce single-serve cup, place 5 ounces of vanilla ice cubes. Add 1½ ounces of frozen all-butter pound cake, cut into 1-inch cubes; 1 ounce of frozen chocolate fudge, cut into 1-inch cubes; and 1 cup of whole milk. Put bladed lid onto cup and blend on single-serve setting for 30 seconds. Carefully remove blades, put on drinking lid, and enjoy.

A rich peanut butter shake that adds peanut butter cookies for a surprise texture and mini crunch in a shake.

peanut butter cookie milkshake

YIELD: 7 cups (56 oz.)
SERVES: 6
PREP TIME: 10 minutes
CALORIES: 377 per 9-oz. serving

• • • • •

ingredients

4 cups vanilla ice cream

½ cup creamy peanut butter

2 cups whole milk

5 ounces peanut butter cookies

• • • • •

mix-in options

PEANUT BUTTER CUPS
SNICKERDOODLE
CHOCOLATE CHIPS

method

For 72-Ounce Blender:

4. In a Ninja 72-ounce pitcher fitted with the standard blade attachment, place the vanilla ice cream. Add the peanut butter, whole milk, and peanut butter cookies. Using the crush function, process for 30 seconds.

5. Remove the lid, carefully remove the blades, and serve.

For Single-Serve Cup:

1. In a Ninja 16-ounce single-serve cup, place 1 ounce of peanut butter cookies, 1 cup of vanilla ice cream, 2 tablespoons of creamy peanut butter and ⅔ cup of whole milk. Put bladed lid onto cup and blend on single-serve setting for 25 seconds. Carefully remove blades, put on drinking lid, and enjoy.

This milkshake will bring back summer memories at your favorite ice cream shop. The perfect accompaniment to a burger and fries.

strawberry milkshake

YIELD: 8 cups (64 oz.)
SERVES: 6
PREP TIME: 10 minutes
CALORIES: 302 per 10-oz. serving

· · · · ·

ingredients

10 ounces whole frozen strawberries

3 cups vanilla ice cream

¾ cup low-sugar strawberry preserves

2¾ cups whole milk

· · · · ·

mix-in options

FROZEN
RASPBERRIES
CHOCOLATE CHIPS

method

For 72-Ounce Blender:

1. In a Ninja 72-ounce pitcher fitted with the standard blade attachment, place the frozen strawberries. Add the vanilla ice cream, low-sugar strawberry preserves and whole milk. Using the crush function, process for 30 seconds.

2. Remove the lid, carefully remove the blades, and serve.

For Single-Serve Cup:

1. In a Ninja 16-ounce single-serve cup, place 2½ ounces of whole frozen strawberries, ¾ cup of vanilla ice cream, 3 tablespoons of low-sugar strawberry preserves, and ¾ cup of whole milk. Put bladed lid onto cup and blend on single-serve setting for 25 seconds. Carefully remove blades, put on drinking lid, and enjoy.

*T**he distinct flavors of cinnamon and nutmeg give this a fall holiday scent and taste. The mini marshmallows add an unexpected treat!***

marshmallow crème milkshake

YIELD: 7 cups (56 oz.)
SERVES: 6
PREP TIME: 12 minutes
CALORIES: 364 per 8-oz. serving

• • • • •

ingredients

1½ cups marshmallow crème

½ teaspoon ground cinnamon

¼ teaspoon ground nutmeg

4 cups vanilla ice cream

1¾ cups whole milk

3 ounces mini marshmallows, frozen

• • • • •

mix-in options

SPRINKLES
PEPPERMINT
PATTIES

method

For 72-Ounce Blender:

1. In a Ninja 72-ounce pitcher fitted with the standard blade attachment, place the marshmallow crème. Add the cinnamon, nutmeg, vanilla ice cream, whole milk, and mini marshmallows. Using the crush function, process for 35 seconds.

2. Remove the lid, carefully remove the blades, and serve.

For Single-Serve Cup:

1. In a Ninja 16-ounce single-serve cup, place ½ ounce of frozen mini marshmallows, 1¼ cups of vanilla ice cream, ⅛ teaspoon of ground cinnamon, a pinch of ground nutmeg, ⅔ cup of whole milk, and ⅓ cup of marshmallow crème. Put bladed lid onto cup and blend on single-serve setting for 25 seconds. Carefully remove blades, put on drinking lid, and enjoy.

D*ulce de leche is made by heating sweetened milk until it caramelizes. When combined with the butterscotch pudding, together they give the unique caramel flavor to this coffee drink.*

dulce de leche coffee drink

YIELD: 6 cups (48 oz.)
SERVES: 4
PREP TIME: 10 minutes
CALORIES: 95 per 12-oz. serving

. . . . .

ingredients

3 cups low-fat milk, divided

1 package (3.4 ounces) butterscotch instant pudding mix

2 cups dark roasted coffee, cold

¼ cup dulce de leche (You can always find dulce de leche in the Mexican food section)

1 teaspoon vanilla extract

. . . . .

method

1. In a large mixing bowl, pour 2 cups of low-fat milk. Add the butterscotch pudding mix into the milk. Lightly whisk the mixture using a wire whisk until dissolved, approximately one minute. Do not overmix or the mixture will thicken and not be easy to pour.

2. Pour the mixture into two standard ice cube trays, equally distributing between the two.

3. Place the ice cube trays in the freezer and freeze for eight hours or overnight.

For 72-Ounce Blender:

4. In a Ninja 72-ounce pitcher fitted with the standard blade attachment, place all the frozen butterscotch ice cubes. Add the remaining 1 cup of low-fat milk, cold coffee, dulce de leche, and the vanilla. Using the crush function, process approximately 35 seconds or until smooth.

5. Remove the lid, carefully remove the blades, and serve.

For Single-Serve Cup:

1. In a Ninja 16-ounce single-serve cup, place 5 ounces of butterscotch ice cubes (¼ of total cubes). Add 4 ounces of cold coffee, 2 ounces of low-fat milk, 1 tablespoon of dulce de leche, and ¼ teaspoon of vanilla. Put bladed lid onto cup and blend on single-serve setting for 20 seconds. Carefully remove blades, put on drinking lid, and enjoy.

*A*ccording to a national taste test, raspberry was the best combination of fruit with coffee. I think you will agree. However, you can follow this same recipe with any of your favorite frozen fruit.

raspberry coffee milkshake

YIELD: 6 cups (48 oz.)
SERVES: 4
PREP TIME: 10 minutes
CALORIES: 189 per 12-oz. serving

· · · · ·

ingredients

2 cups whole milk

1 12-ounce package frozen unsweetened raspberries

3 cups dark roasted coffee, cold

1 package (3.4 ounces) vanilla instant pudding mix

2 tablespoons agave nectar

· · · · ·

method

1. In a large mixing bowl, pour the whole milk. Add the vanilla pudding mix into the milk. Lightly whisk the mixture using a wire whisk until dissolved, approximately one minute. Do not overmix or the mixture will thicken and not be easy to pour.

2. Pour the mixture into two standard ice cube trays, equally distributing between the two.

3. Place the ice cube trays in the freezer and freeze for eight hours or overnight.

For 72-Ounce Blender:

4. In a Ninja 72-ounce pitcher fitted with the standard blade attachment, place all the frozen vanilla ice cubes. Add the cold coffee, raspberries, and agave nectar. Using the pulse function, pulse until cubes and frozen raspberries are well mixed, then set to crush and blend approximately 60 seconds or until smooth.

5. Remove the lid, carefully remove the blades, and serve.

For Single-Serve Cup:

1. In a Ninja 16-ounce single-serve cup, place 5 ounces of vanilla ice cubes (¼ of total cubes). Add 6 ounces of cold coffee, 3 ounces of frozen raspberries, and ½ tablespoon of agave nectar. Put bladed lid onto cup and blend on single-serve setting for 30 seconds. Carefully remove blades, put on drinking lid, and enjoy.

C hocolate and coffee been popular since they were first paired together hundreds of years ago. The coconut added to this shake give it the taste of a popular candy bar.

chocolate coconut iced coffee milkshake

YIELD: 6 cups (48 oz.)
SERVES: 4
PREP TIME: 10 minutes
CALORIES: 149 per 12-oz. serving

• • • • •

ingredients

2 cups coconut milk

1 package (3.4 ounces) chocolate instant pudding mix

3½ cups dark roasted coffee, cold

2 tablespoons coconut extract

2 tablespoons agave nectar

• • • • •

method

1. In a large mixing bowl, pour the coconut milk. Add the chocolate pudding mix into the milk. Lightly whisk the mixture using a wire whisk until dissolved, approximately one minute. Do not overmix or the mixture will thicken and not be easy to pour.

2. Pour the mixture into two standard ice cube trays, equally distributing between the two.

3. Place the ice cube trays in the freezer and freeze for eight hours or overnight.

For 72-Ounce Blender:

4. In a Ninja 72-ounce pitcher fitted with the standard blade attachment, place all the frozen coconut chocolate ice cubes. Add 3½ cups of cold coffee, coconut extract, and agave nectar. Using the crush function, blend approximately 35 seconds or until smooth.

5. Remove the lid, carefully remove the blades, and serve.

For Single-Serve Cup:

1. In a Ninja 16-ounce single-serve cup, place 5 ounces of coconut chocolate ice cubes (¼ of total cubes). Add 7.5 ounces of cold coffee, ½ tablespoon of coconut extract, and ½ tablespoon of agave nectar. Put bladed lid onto cup and blend on single-serve setting for 30 seconds. Carefully remove blades, put on drinking lid, and enjoy!

C hocolate, hazelnut, and coffee make for a winning combination and will add variety to any coffee lover's coffee shake addiction. You can also make this with whole, low-fat, or skim milk using the same proportions.

hazelnut chocolate coffee soy milkshake

YIELD: 6 cups (48 oz.)
SERVES: 4
PREP TIME: 10 minutes
CALORIES: 118 per 12-oz. serving

· · · · ·

ingredients

3 cups soy milk, divided

2 cups dark roasted coffee, cold

1 package (3.4 ounces) chocolate instant pudding mix

¼ cup hazelnut-flavored creamer

· · · · ·

method

1. In a large mixing bowl, pour 2 cups of soy milk. Add the chocolate pudding mix into the milk. Lightly whisk the mixture using a wire whisk until dissolved, approximately one minute. Do not overmix or the mixture will thicken and not be easy to pour.

2. Pour the mixture into two standard ice cube trays, equally distributing between the two.

3. Place the ice cube trays in the freezer and freeze for eight hours or overnight.

For 72-Ounce Blender:

4. In a Ninja 72-ounce pitcher fitted with the standard blade attachment, place all the frozen chocolate ice cubes. Add the remaining 1 cup of soy milk, the cold coffee, and the hazelnut-flavored creamer. Using the crush function, process approximately 35 seconds or until smooth.

5. Remove the lid, carefully remove the blades, and serve.

For Single-Serve Cup:

1. In a Ninja 16-ounce single-serve cup, place 5 ounces of chocolate ice cubes (¼ of total cubes). Add 4 ounces of cold coffee, ¼ cup of soy milk, and 1 ounce of hazelnut-flavored creamer. Put bladed lid onto cup and blend on single-serve setting for 30 seconds. Carefully remove blades, put on drinking lid, and enjoy.

Acai Blueberry Sorbet, 126

sorbets & ices

lemon water ice 123

mango guanabana sorbet 125

bellini water ice 126

acai blueberry sorbet 126

chunky sangria sorbet 127

grapefruit honey water ice. 128

watermelon lemonade water ice. 129

cherry cola water ice 130

cantaloupe white grape sorbet 131

T his treat is really tart, so add an extra tablespoon of honey if you like it sweeter.

lemon water ice

YIELD: 2 cups
SERVES: 4
PREP TIME: 6 minutes
CALORIES: 80

· · · · ·

ingredients

2 lemons, peeled, cut into quarters

13 ounces lemonade

2 tablespoons honey

· · · · ·

method

1. Place lemons, lemonade, and honey into the Ninja food processor and process for 30 seconds. Carefully remove blade.

2. Strain mixture into a bowl. Discard pulp.

3. Pour liquid into ice cube trays and freeze overnight until solid.

4. When frozen, place ice cubes into the food-processing bowl and process for 20 seconds, or until desired consistency is achieved.

*I*f you haven't heard of the latest health craze of guanabana, also known as graiola or sour sop, you soon will as it is becoming very popular and is already available with at least eight brands in America. It has a unique flavor and, when combined with the mango, is delicious.

mango guanabana sorbet

YIELD: 1¼ pints
SERVES: 6
PREP TIME: 2 minutes
CALORIES: 72 per 4-oz. serving

• • • • •

ingredients

1 pound frozen mango chunks

1 cup plus 2 tablespoons guanabana (sour sop) nectar, cold

• • • • •

method

1. In a Ninja 56-ounce food-processing bowl fitted with the standard blade attachment, place the frozen mango chunks. Add the guanabana nectar. Using the crush function, process for 25 seconds.

2. Remove the lid, carefully remove the blades, and serve.

This peach-flavored bellini has been a favorite frozen cocktail, now revised to become a water ice.

bellini water ice

YIELD: 2 pints
SERVES: 8
PREP TIME: 10 minutes
CALORIES: 57 per 4-oz. serving

· · · · ·

ingredients

10 ounces frozen peach slices

14 ounces peach nectar

6 ounces prosecco, cold

method

1. Place the frozen peach slices, peach nectar, and prosecco in the Ninja 72-ounce pitcher and crush for 25 seconds.

2. Pour the mixture into two standard ice cube trays, equally distributing between the two.

3. Place the ice cube trays in the freezer and freeze for eight hours or overnight.

4. In a Ninja 56-ounce food-processing bowl fitted with the standard blade attachment, place all the frozen peach cubes. Using the crush function, process for 25 seconds.

5. Remove the lid, carefully remove the blades, and serve.

· ·

Acai berry is thought of by many in the health food field as a "superfood." Health benefits aside, it is berry, berry good!

acai blueberry sorbet

YIELD: 1½ pints
SERVES: 6
PREP TIME: 2 minutes
CALORIES: 80 per 4-oz. serving

· · · · ·

ingredients

1¼ pounds frozen blueberries

2 tablespoons granulated sugar

1 cup acai juice, cold

method

1. In a Ninja 56-ounce food-processing bowl fitted with the standard blade attachment, place the frozen blueberries. Dissolve the granulated sugar in the acai juice, then add to food-processing bowl. Using the crush function, process for 40 seconds.

2. Remove the lid, carefully remove the blades, and serve.

T his recipe was voted the tastiest sorbet by our panel of tasters. It has a really rich, vibrant complex flavor with a clean finish after every bite.

chunky sangria sorbet

SERVES: 50 ounces
PREP TIME: 4 minutes
CALORIES: 108 per 4-oz. serving

· · · · ·

ingredients

6 ounces frozen pineapple chunks

6 ounces frozen mango chunks

6 ounces frozen whole strawberries

6 ounces frozen peach slices

2 tablespoons granulated sugar

3 cups plus 2 tablespoons red wine, cold

2 tablespoons brandy, cold

· · · · ·

method

1. In a Ninja 56-ounce food-processing bowl fitted with the standard blade attachment, place the frozen pineapple chunks, mango chunks, strawberries, and peach slices. Dissolve the granulated sugar in the red wine, then add to the processing bowl. Add brandy. Using the crush function, process for one minute.

2. Remove the lid, carefully remove the blades, and serve.

This is the perfect sorbet to serve after a fish course. It is a great, refreshing palate cleanser.

grapefruit honey water ice

YIELD: 2 pints
SERVES: 8
PREP TIME: 10 minutes
CALORIES: 64 per 4-oz. serving

· · · · ·

ingredients

2¼ cups grapefruit juice, divided

12 ounces fresh grapefruit segments

¼ cup honey

· · · · ·

method

1. Place 2 cups of grapefruit juice, grapefruit segments, and honey in the Ninja 72-ounce pitcher and crush for 20 seconds.

2. Pour the mixture into two standard ice cube trays, equally distributing between the two.

3. Place the ice cube trays in the freezer and freeze for eight hours or overnight.

4. In a Ninja 56-ounce food-processing bowl fitted with the standard blade attachment, place all the frozen grapefruit cubes and the remaining ¼ cup of grapefruit juice. Using the crush function, process for 30 seconds.

5. Remove the lid, carefully remove the blades, and serve.

W atermelon and lemonade are everyone's
summertime favorites. You will love the two flavors
combined in this cold mouth-freshening delight.

watermelon lemonade water ice

YIELD: 2 pints
SERVES: 6
PREP TIME: 10 minutes
CALORIES: 51 per 4-oz. serving

· · · · ·

ingredients

**1½ pounds fresh
watermelon, cut into
pieces**

1 cup lemonade

**2 tablespoons
lemon zest**

· · · · ·

method

1. Place the fresh watermelon pieces, lemonade, and lemon zest in the Ninja 72-ounce pitcher and crush for 20 seconds.

2. Pour the mixture into two standard ice cube trays, equally distributing between the two.

3. Place the ice cube trays in the freezer and freeze for eight hours or overnight.

4. In a Ninja 56-ounce food-processing bowl fitted with the standard blade attachment, place all the frozen watermelon lemonade cubes. Using the crush function, process for 35 seconds.

5. Remove the lid, carefully remove the blades, and serve.

The combination of cherry and cola with a lime on the glass was always a soda fountain favorite. It makes a refreshing water ice, too.

cherry cola water ice

YIELD: 2 pints
SERVES: 8
PREP TIME: 10 minutes
CALORIES: 51 per 4-oz. serving

· · · · ·

ingredients

12 ounces frozen dark sweet cherries

16-ounces cola

1 lime, peeled, cut in half

· · · · ·

method

1. Place the frozen dark sweet cherries, cola, and lime halves in the Ninja 72-ounce pitcher and crush for 45 seconds.

2. Pour the mixture into two standard ice cube trays, equally distributing between the two.

3. Place the ice cube trays in the freezer and freeze for eight hours or overnight.

4. In a Ninja 56-ounce food-processing bowl fitted with the standard blade attachment, place all the frozen cherry cola cubes. Using the crush function, process for 25 seconds.

5. Remove the lid, carefully remove the blades, and serve.

C antaloupe's texture is ideal for making a sorbet, but it's a bit sweet by itself. The addition of the white grape juice gives it the bit of acid and tang it needs to really be good.

cantaloupe white grape sorbet

YIELD: 1½ pints
SERVES: 6
PREP TIME: 10 minutes
CALORIES: 69 per 4-oz. serving

• • • • •

ingredients

1 pound fresh cantaloupe, peeled, seeded, cut into pieces

1 cup white grape juice

2 tablespoons sugar substitute

• • • • •

method

1. Place the cut cantaloupe into ice cube trays or onto a sheet pan spread out evenly so that each piece can freeze individually and not clump together. Freeze for eight hours or overnight.

2. In a small mixing bowl, pour white grape juice. Add the sugar substitute and mix until dissolved.

3. In a Ninja 56-ounce food-processing bowl fitted with the standard blade attachment, place all the frozen cantaloupe pieces and white grape juice sugar substitute mixture. Using the crush function, process for 35 seconds.

4. Remove the lid, carefully remove the blades, and serve.

6 pops

mango pineapple ice pops 134

blueberry limeade ice pops 134

watermelon ice pops 135

mixed-berry ice pops 136

raspberry apple ice pops 137

strawberry ice pops 137

cookies & cream pudding pops 138

dirt pudding pops 139

peanut butter banana pudding pops 140

white chocolate chip pistachio pudding pops 140

sweet strawberries & cream pudding pops 141

creamy pineapple-orange yogurt pops 142

*M*ango and pineapple make this a really tropical treat. With the addition of the agave nectar, it is still only 80 calories per pop.

mango pineapple ice pops

YIELD: 24 ounces
SERVES: 6 to 8 pops
PREP TIME: 11 minutes
CALORIES: 80 per 3-oz. pop

· · · · · ·

ingredients

1 cup frozen mangoes

2 cups frozen pineapple chunks

2 tablespoons agave nectar (more or less to taste)

method

1. Place all of the ingredients into a Ninja Blender and blend for one minute or until smooth.
2. Pour fruit puree in small ice pop molds.
3. Freeze for three to six hours until hard.

· ·

*B*lueberries are often recognized as a "superfood." This can be an even healthier treat if you substitute agave nectar or honey for the sugar.

blueberry limeade ice pops

YIELD: 21 ounces
SERVES: 5 to 7 pops
PREP TIME: 10 minutes
CALORIES: 82 per 3-oz. pop

· · · · · ·

ingredients

12 ounces frozen blueberries

¾ cup sugar, or to taste

½ cup water

⅓ cup fresh lime juice

method

1. Place all of the ingredients into a Ninja blender and blend for approximately one minute or until smooth.
2. Pour ingredients into small ice pop molds and freeze for three to six hours until hard.

E njoy watermelon on a stick with chocolate chip sprinkles. What a great snack on a hot day!

watermelon ice pops

YIELD: 34 ounces
SERVES: 6 to 10 pops
PREP TIME: 10 minutes
CALORIES: 99 per 3-oz. pop

· · · · ·

ingredients

**1½ lbs. seedless
watermelon without
the rind, cut into
pieces**

**2 tablespoons
sugar**

**2 teaspoons
lemon zest**

pinch of salt

**1 cup chocolate chips
or chunks**

· · · · ·

method

1. In a Ninja 56-ounce food-processing bowl, place watermelon, sugar, lemon zest, and salt. Process for 45 seconds until smooth, remove blades.

2. With a spatula, gently stir chocolate chips or chunks into the mixture, distributing evenly.

3. Spoon mixture into ice pop molds.

4. Freeze for three to six hours until hard. Enjoy!

M ost supermarkets carry this very popular combination of berries in the frozen-fruit section. If your market doesn't carry this combination, you can always purchase each berry separately. It will be worth it.

mixed-berry ice pops

YIELD: 26 ounces
SERVES: 6 to 8 pops
PREP TIME: 10 minutes
CALORIES: 92 per 3-oz. pop

. . . . . .

ingredients

1 package 16-ounce frozen mixed berries (blueberry, raspberry, and strawberry)

¾ cup sugar, or to taste

⅓ cup water

¼ cup fresh lemon juice

. . . . . .

method

1. Add all of the ingredients to a Ninja blender and process until smooth, about two minutes.

2. Pour into ice pop molds and freeze for three to six hours until hard.

R aspberry and apple are an unusual combination that really works. The agave nectar makes this an all-natural treat!

raspberry apple ice pops

YIELD: 21 ounces
SERVES: 5 to 7 pops
PREP TIME: 11 minutes
CALORIES: 50 per 3-oz. pop

· · · · · ·

ingredients

1 package 12-ounce frozen raspberries

¾ cup apple juice

2 tablespoons agave nectar

method

1. Place all of the ingredients in a Ninja blender and blend for one minute or until smooth.

2. Pour puree into ice pop molds and freeze for three to six hours until hard.

T hese strawberry ice pops are easy to make. What makes these colorful pops unique and interesting is the spooned-in chopped strawberries that give these pops their special look and texture.

strawberry ice pops

YIELD: 21 ounces
SERVES: 5 to 7 pops
PREP TIME: 11 minutes
CALORIES: 105 per 3-oz. pop

· · · · · ·

ingredients

2 cups frozen strawberries

2 tablespoons fresh lemon juice

½ cup confectioners sugar (to taste)

½ cup finely chopped strawberries, set aside

method

1. In a Ninja 56-ounce food-processing bowl fitted with the standard blade attachment, place all ingredients (excluding finely chopped strawberries) and puree until smooth.

2. Divide finely chopped strawberries evenly into ice pop molds, then spoon berry mixture evenly into each mold.

3. Freeze for three to six hours until hard.

E verybody likes cookies and cream ice cream. It is even more fun frozen into a pop, because you get to have a chewy crunch between licks and bites.

cookies & cream pudding pops

YIELD: 24 ounces
SERVES: 6 to 8 pops
PREP TIME: 11 minutes
CALORIES: 68 per 3-oz. pop

• • • • •

ingredients

2 cups whole milk

**1 package
(4.2 ounces) cookies
and cream instant
pudding mix**

**3.5 ounces mini Oreo®
bite-size cookies**

• • • • •

method

1. In a Ninja 56-ounce food-processing bowl fitted with the standard blade attachment, add the whole milk and the cookies and cream instant pudding mix.

2. Divide mini Oreo® cookies evenly into ice pop molds, then spoon in pudding mix into each mold.

3. Freeze for three to six hours until hard. Enjoy!

W on't your kids be surprised eating dirt pudding pops and finding a worm!

dirt pudding pops

YIELD: 8 pops
SERVES: 6 to 10 pops
PREP TIME: 10 minutes
CALORIES: 145 per 3-oz. pop

· · · · · ·

ingredients

2 cups whole milk

1 package (4.2 ounces) chocolate instant pudding mix

3.5 ounces chocolate graham crackers

4 tablespoons melted butter

16 gummy worms

· · · · · ·

method

1. In a Ninja 56-ounce food-processing bowl, place the chocolate graham crackers. Pulse until crushed. Pour in the melted butter and mix. Remove blades from bowl.

2. In a large mixing bowl pour the whole milk. Add the chocolate pudding mix into the milk. Lightly whisk the mixture using a wire whisk until dissolved, approximately one minute. Do not overmix or the mixture will thicken and not be easy to pour.

3. Spoon approximately ½ tablespoon graham cracker mixture into the top of each mold. Pressing slightly to compact the mixture, press a gummy worm into the mixture and spoon the pudding mix into the mold leaving room at the bottom end for another ½ tablespoon of graham cracker mixture and another gummy worm.

4. Freeze for three to six hours until hard.

P eanut butter and bananas go together in shakes, ice cream, and especially in this delicious pop.

peanut butter banana pudding pops

YIELD: 1½ pints
SERVES: 6 to 10 pops
PREP TIME: 11 minutes
CALORIES: 159 per 3-oz. pop

· · · · · ·

ingredients

¾ **cup creamy peanut butter**

2 cups whole milk

1 package (3.4 ounces) vanilla instant pudding mix

2 whole bananas, sliced to ¼-inch thick

method

1. In a Ninja 56-ounce food-processing bowl fitted with the standard blade attachment, add the peanut butter and the whole milk. Blend thoroughly. Add vanilla instant pudding mix and blend for 30 seconds.

2. Fill ice pop molds approximately two-third full.

3. Drop several banana slices into each ice pop mold until the mold is full. Insert ice pop stick/handle into each mold.

4. Freeze for three to six hours until hard. Enjoy!

· ·

P istachio has become a ice cream and pudding favorite. This pop enhances the flavor with white chocolate chips and adds crunch with the chopped pistachios.

white chocolate chip pistachio pudding pops

YIELD: 28 ounces
SERVES: 6 to 10 pops
PREP TIME: 11 minutes
CALORIES: 145 per 3-oz. pop

· · · · · ·

ingredients

2 cups whole milk

1 package (4.2 ounces) pistachio instant pudding mix

½ cup white chocolate chips

½ cup chopped pistachio nuts

method

1. In a Ninja 56-ounce food-processing bowl fitted with the standard blade attachment, add the whole milk and the pistachio instant pudding mix. Blend thoroughly and pour into mixing bowl.

2. Fold white chocolate chips and chopped nuts into pudding mixture until blended.

3. Pour mixture into the ice pop molds.

4. Freeze for three to six hours until hard.

S trawberry popsicles are a great treat in the summer when you need a refreshment in the sun!

sweet strawberries & cream pudding pops

YIELD: 34 ounces
SERVES: 6 to 10 pops
PREP TIME: 10 minutes
CALORIES: 80 per 3-oz. pop

· · · · ·

ingredients

2 cups (12 ounces) of strawberries (fresh or frozen)

2 tablespoons honey

2 cups whole milk

1 package (3.4 ounces) vanilla instant pudding mix

· · · · ·

method

1. In a Ninja 56-ounce food-processing bowl place the strawberries and the honey, and blend until smooth.

2. In a large mixing bowl, pour the whole milk. Add the vanilla pudding mix into the milk. Lightly whisk the mixture using a wire whisk until dissolved, approximately one minute. Do not overmix or the mixture will thicken and not be easy to pour.

3. For each mold, first fill the mold one-third full of pudding mixture. Then layer in 1 tablespoon of the strawberry puree. Add remaining pudding mixture evenly to fill the mold. Place ice pop stick in each mold.

4. Freeze for three to six hours until hard.

Why not make a pop that tastes great and is healthier, too? The combination of low-fat yogurt, pineapples, and agave nectar does just that.

creamy pineapple-orange yogurt pops

YIELD: 30 ounces
SERVES: 6 to 10 pops
PREP TIME: 10 minutes
CALORIES: 64 per 3-oz. pop

· · · · · ·

ingredients

12 ounces frozen pineapples

1 cup orange juice

1 cup plain low-fat yogurt

2 teaspoons vanilla extract

1 tablespoon agave nectar

method

1. Add all of the ingredients to a Ninja blender and blend for one minute or until smooth.

2. Pour puree into ice pop molds and freeze for three to six hours until hard.

ice cream

a hun-ny of coffee ice cream, 67
basic chocolate ice cream, 12
basic vanilla ice cream, 13
black & white grasshopper pie ice cream, 45
blueberry lemon shortcake ice cream, 54
butterscotch rocky road ice cream, 59
cake batter ice cream, 58
cannoli ice cream, 35
caramel pretzel ice cream, 19
chocolate brownie heaven ice cream, 49
chocolate caramel pecan pie ice cream, 42
chocolate cherry cake ice cream, 33
chocolate hazelnut ice cream, 29
chocolate orange ice cream, 65
chocolate peanut butter ice cream, 37
chocolate truffle ice cream, 50
cinnamon buns ice cream, 48
coconut almond ice cream, 61
coconut rum raisin ice cream, 31
cookies & cream chocolate cheesecake
    ice cream, 63
cookies & cream ice cream, 38
crispety crunchety peanut butter
    ice cream, 23
crunchy banana strawberry granola
    ice cream, 25
dulce de leche cheesecake ice cream, 57
dulce de leche ice cream, 44
hawaiian ice cream, 27
hot chocolate marshmallow ice cream, 43
key lime lemon pie ice cream, 60
the kitchen sink ice cream, 52
loaded pistachio ice cream, 66
mexican chocolate ice cream, 41
mint chocolate ice cream, 40
oatmeal cookie ice cream, 56
peach cobbler ice cream, 55
peanut butter cream pie ice cream
piña colada ice cream, 17
pineapple upside-down cake ice cream, 47
pistachio macaroon ice cream, 21
pistachio rice pudding ice cream, 62
pomegranate nuts & spice ice cream, 53
pumpkin cheesecake ice cream, 46
s'mores ice cream, 15
strawberry cheesecake ice cream, 39
tiramisu ice cream, 64
white chocolate malted ice cream, 36
white chocolate orange creamsicle
    ice cream, 34

fruit-based ice cream

blueberry rice pudding ice cream, 79
chocolate-coated cherry ice cream, 77
paradise punch ice cream, 71
peach ice cream, 73
peachy cheesecake ice cream, 74
pineapple caramel ice cream, 76
strawberry ice cream, 78
tropical burst ice cream, 75

low-calorie d'lites

banana maple ice cream, 83
cafè mocha chip ice cream, 85
cherries jubilee ice cream, 94
chocolate candy ice cream, 95
italian cookie ice cream, 96
lemon ginger snap bar ice cream, 87
mixed berry smoothie ice cream, 89
my favorite frozen yogurt, 97
raspberry rush sorbet, 91
snickerdoodle cookie ice cream, 93

milkshakes & coffee drinks

bananas foster milkshake, 110
boston cream pie milkshake, 112
caramel éclair milkshake, 103
cherry cheesecake milkshake, 105
chocolate coconut iced-coffee
    milkshake, 118
dulce de leche coffee drink, 116
hazelnut chocolate coffee soy
    milkshake, 119
malted milkshake, 109
marshmallow créme milkshake, 115
mint cookies & cream milkshake, 101
mocha chocolate milkshake, 107
peanut butter cookie milkshake, 113,
pistachio rocky road milkshake, 111
pumpkin coffee milkshake, 108
raspberry coffee milkshake, 117
strawberry milkshake, 114

sorbets & ices

acai blueberry sorbet, 126
bellini water ice, 126
cantaloupe white grape sorbet, 131
cherry cola water ice, 130
chunky sangria sorbet, 127
grapefruit honey water ice, 128
lemon water ice, 123
mango guanabana sorbet, 125
watermelon lemonade water ice, 129

pops

blueberry limeade ice pops, 134
cookies & cream pudding pops, 138
creamy pineapple-orange yogurt pops, 142
dirt pudding pops, 139
mango pineapple ice pops, 134
mixed-berry ice pops, 136
peanut butter banana pudding pops, 140
raspberry apple ice pops, 137
strawberry ice pops, 137
sweet strawberries & cream pudding
    pops, 141
watermelon ice pops, 135
white chocolate chip pistachio pudding
    pops, 140

101
frozen, decadent
desserts,
drinks & treats

RULE THE KITCHEN®